THE TASTE OF OUR TIME

Collection planned and directed by

ALBERT SKIRA

BIOGRAPHICAL AND CRITICAL STUDY

BY

GIULIO CARLO ARGAN

Curator General of Fine Arts in Italy

Translated from the Italian by James Emmons

FRA ANGELICO

SKIRA

Title Page:
Angel's Head, detail from the Coronation of the Virgin.
Ca. 1430-1440. Louvre, Paris.

Library of Congress Catalog Card Number: 55-7700.

FRA ANGELICO AND HIS TIMES

★

HIS LIFE

THE MAN AND THE ARTIST
IN THE LIGHT OF CRITICAL TRADITION

HIS AESTHETIC

HIS LIFE

GIOVANNI da Fiesole, better known as Fra Angelico, has often been held up, especially by the romantics, as the prototype of the mystic artist rapt in the contemplation of ineffable visions, which he painted in spells of blissful piety. There is no denying that he was a man of saintly habits, a learned and zealous friar, a spiritual-minded painter if ever there was one. Yet his art arose within the complex of trends that shaped 15th-century Florentine art, and logically remained within them, just as its sacred content stemmed directly from the religious doctrines of his day. Though it expounded the most orthodox traditions of Catholic thought, his spiritual message is no less well-defined and self-conscious than that —however different—which was voiced in the works of those early 15th-century masters whose achievements we call the Renaissance. He himself was very much a man of the Renaissance, a cultural revolution in which he played no small part, even though he sought to enlist it in the service of purely religious ends, exalting the humanitarian values of Christianity instead of those attaching to classical Antiquity.

Born in 1387 near the castle of Vicchio in the upper valley of the Mugello, not far from Florence, Guido di Pietro (i.e. Guido, son of Pietro) was a youth of twenty when, in 1407, he and his brother presented themselves at the Dominican convent of the Observance at Fiesole (the Observant convents were those in which the strictest Rule was observed). After a year's noviciate at Cortona, he returned to Fiesole in 1408 and took the cowl for good under the name of Fra Giovanni. These were years of schism and dissension in the Church, and

◄ THE LAST JUDGMENT, THE ASCENSION AND PENTECOST, DETAIL FROM THE LEFT PANEL. CA. 1450. GALLERIA NAZIONALE D'ARTE ANTICA, ROME.

Florence, after backing Gregory XII for a time, shifted its allegiance to the Antipope Alexander V in 1409. As they remained loyal to the Roman Pope Gregory XII, the Dominican monks were expelled from Fiesole by the Florentine government; they took refuge first at Foligno, then at Cortona. Only in 1418, the Council of Constance having at last healed the Great Schism and elected a new pope, Martin V, could they return to their monastery at Fiesole. Fra Giovanni may be assumed to have shared these years of exile, during which, very probably, he served his apprenticeship as an illuminator and fresco-painter. What is certain is that his contacts with Florentine art life did not begin until 1418.

Records of the time make no mention of him as a painter until many years later. In 1432 the Order of the Servites at Brescia commissioned an *Annunciation* from him. In 1433, at Florence, the Compagnia dei Linaiuoli (the flax-makers' guild) called him in to paint a large altarpiece, for which Lorenzo Ghiberti designed the marble frame. In 1438, writing to Piero de' Medici from Perugia, Domenico Veneziano recommended him as one of the best painters in Florence.

In 1436 the Observant monks left Fiesole for the convent of San Marco at Florence, rebuilt especially for them by Cosimo de' Medici. Fra Giovanni was asked to paint two pictures for the convent church and to decorate the chapter house, refectory, hospice, cloisters and cells with frescos. In 1437 he painted an altarpiece for the church of San Domenico at Perugia.

Though his fame as a painter overshadowed the fact, he had also risen to a position of authority within the Order. We can hardly credit the story echoed by Vasari, who tells how in 1445 the Pope offered to make him archbishop of Florence; but Fra Giovanni, with his accustomed modesty, declined in favor of a fellow friar, later known as St Antoninus. The esteem and consideration he enjoyed in papal circles, however, is shown by his being called to Rome to decorate the Chapel of Nicholas V at the Vatican. The earliest mention of these frescos dates from 1447, and also refers to the assistance given him by several other artists, amongst them Benozzo Gozzoli. That same year, by written contract, he agreed to decorate the chapel of San Brizio in Orvieto Cathedral; he made no more than a beginning, however, and these frescos were completed many years later by Luca Signorelli.

The frescos at the Vatican kept him busy until 1449, when he was appointed Prior of the convent of San Marco, and held office for three years. In 1452 he was discussing terms for the decoration of a chapel in Prato Cathedral. He may have been recalled to Rome in 1454, where in any case he is known to have died in 1455, at the age of sixty-eight. Bearing an epitaph in humanist Latin, his tomb may still be seen in Santa Maria sopra Minerva in Rome.

Angelico was the name bestowed on Fra Giovanni by his fellow monks, but not—as Vasari would have us believe—because his paintings seemed worthier of angels than of men. If, as will be presently shown, his painting is solidly grounded on Catholic tenets and may in a sense be regarded as a peculiar exposition of the aesthetic principles laid down two centuries earlier by St Thomas Aquinas, the "Angelical Doctor," we need not be surprised at finding him called the "Angelical Painter," i.e. the Aquinas of painting. This is but one more reason to read into his art not the visions of an inspired mystic, but the devout offerings of a highly gifted artist, fully conscious of his powers.

THE MAN AND THE ARTIST
IN THE LIGHT OF CRITICAL TRADITION

IF so stubborn a tissue of legend clings to the figure of Fra
Angelico, Vasari is chiefly to blame. Here, in a nutshell, is
what he has to say: Fra Angelico was a saint, hence his painting
is saintly; he never took up his brush without first praying
intently and weeping abundant tears, hence his paintings reflect
the heavenly visions glimpsed in these fits of ecstasy, and therefore are his faces divinely beautiful, his colors harmonious,
his forms infused with grace and gentleness.

In his biography of Masaccio, citing the painters who owed
their mature style to the frescos in the Brancacci Chapel, Vasari
put Fra Angelico at the top of the list; this was his way of
admitting that the latter was familiar with the most advanced
trends of Quattrocento art. But when he comes to Fra Angelico's
own biography, no mention is made of any such debt, since
obviously, if his painting is divinely inspired, there is no point
in assigning it to historical sources. In the same chapter Vasari
seizes the opportunity to discourse at length on the nature of
religious painting, which, he would have us note, may well be
devout without being insipid, just as a beautiful figure is not
necessarily sensual. He then goes on to question the advisability
of representing nudes in the churches, though these, he grants,
are a great test of the artist's skill. Lionello Venturi (*Pretesti di
Critica*, Hoepli, Milan, 1929, p. 71) has pointed out that this
passage, which appears only in the second edition of Vasari's
Lives (1568), is simply a restatement of the sly objections made
by Aretino to Michelangelo's *Last Judgment* in the Sistine
Chapel. This gives Vasari away, his disquisition on the nude
having nothing to do with Fra Angelico; it was occasioned
simply by the hardly veiled threats of the Counter-Reformation
to clamp down on the freedom of expression artists enjoyed.

For Vasari had realized that not only the profane charms of painting, but the whole aesthetic ideal of the Renaissance stood to suffer at the hands of such bigoted censureship. And he, with a sense of opportunism no less keen than Aretino's, hastened forward with minor concessions intended to salvage the essential. His biography of Fra Angelico reads like the apology of a saint for purely polemical reasons. Fra Angelico being a saintly man, he says, no less pure and saintly is his painting, for all its lovely grace of form, for all its crystalline color. How is it possible, he appeals at the last, for this exultation in the beauties of nature to clash with the religious ideal? But all his arguments were provoked simply by the shrewd realization that the ideals of art Fra Angelico stood for were practically identical with his own, with those, that is, which he was defending against the cold monster of Counter-Reformation morality.

For Vasari, then, the trend of Fra Angelico's art clearly lay in the direction of naturalism, though nature merely excited his admiration for the infinite greatness of God's works and was never the scene of human action and endeavor. Not until Filippo Baldinucci in the 17th century, and Luigi Lanzi in the 18th, made the first systematic attempt to sort out the Italian schools of painting, did Fra Angelico take his rightful place in the rise of Florentine painting. Lanzi pointed out that his is none the less a place apart in that school and, while putting him down as the last of the Giotteschi, he detected something in his painting—perhaps a shade of strain or rhetoric in the grace of his figures—that brings to mind Guido Reni.

The romantic critics of the 19th century relapsed into the old interpretation. Wackenroder and Montalembert saw only the mystic ecstatically painting between spells of divine revelation. Embroidering on Lanzi's reference to the Giotteschi—only one man's opinion, but an historically valid one at any rate—Rio finally converted it into a "mystical school" of

Quattrocento painters, which of course never existed. Then A.W. Schlegel objected that even the most inspired mystic, if he wants to paint satisfactorily, is bound to fall back on actual visual experience; that Fra Angelico was peculiarly adept at handling perspective, well integrated his figures into space, struck light from the contrast with shadow, and brought out form through color, which is but a variation of light. Ruskin went even further when he observed that light is the vital principle behind Fra Angelico's vision, that even his shadows are luminous and dark masses colored. Ruskin laid the basis at last for an objective critical appraisal of this art. For the great contribution of Fra Angelico to Quattrocento art lay precisely in the purely theoretical value he attached to light. If the sustained efforts of Father Marchese in the 19th century to show the link between Fra Angelico's painting and the doctrines of St Thomas Aquinas had borne more analytically on its formal values, he might have realized that this pretended "Thomism" is a matter of style rather than content.

Those who in recent times have sought to throw light on the historical figure of Fra Angelico have either neglected the pious monk that he certainly was, or merely accepted the traditional view of him in this respect. Modern investigations have centered on sifting out the works that are actually his from those of his pupils and followers, on elucidating the mystery in which his formative years are shrouded, and on dating his works in accordance with their stylistic evolution. One problem of interest still hangs fire, however. Granted—and this it is only reasonable to grant—that Fra Angelico was not a wonder-struck mystic given to fits of ecstasy, but a painter well aware of the historical mission of his art. Then, we are entitled to wonder, may not this mission have been largely determined in his own mind by the force, depth and topical character of the religious beliefs he all his life entertained?

HIS AESTHETIC

WE know next to nothing of Fra Angelico's earliest work. Where and with whom he actually studied has never been ascertained. Perhaps the boldest hypothesis—and the most tempting—is that put forward by Roberto Longhi: before Masaccio, he says, Fra Angelico the painter did not exist. That he was not precocious is an accepted fact, and however uncertain the chronology of his early works, none can reasonably be dated prior to 1425. Though the little we know hardly warrants our linking him directly with Masaccio, there is no denying that his entire work arose in terms of the main trends that were then revolutionizing Florentine art, and occasionally conflicted with them. His work, moreover, presupposes a thoroughgoing initiation into Thomist theory that sufficiently accounts for its late beginnings and its doctrinarian character. From the outset his painting adopted a "modern" idiom of expression whereby he acknowledged the sweeping changes coming over art and, instead of contending against them, strove rather to reconcile them with the religious and didactic ends art had traditionally served. But this was not all. At the same time he dreamt of an exhilarating revival of faith, of a triumphant return to the fountainheads of Christian thought. Thus he could hardly remain indifferent to the fresh light in which history was then being reviewed, and the efforts being made to get back to its true sources. For him, however, true history was religious history and the ultimate goal of man's life was the salvation of his soul.

When dealing with Fra Angelico's spiritual outlook, we must never lose sight of the fact that he was not only a Dominican monk, but a venerated, high-ranking member of his Order, which, precisely at that time, was ardently setting up as the spiritual guide of Christendom and bending every effort to consolidate the moral authority of the Church. There is no point in separating Fra Angelico's religious ideals from those of the Dominican Order, especially when the Church herself, paying homage to both the man and the artist, has beatified him, raising him into the elect company of such great contemporary Dominicans as St Catherine of Siena, St Antoninus, Giovanni Dominici and Savonarola. His is religious painting if any is, yet strictly speaking it is ecclesiastical and monastic.

We have touched on the theoretical basis and the propagandist intent that underlie his art. By the former is meant the teaching of St Thomas Aquinas, of which the Dominican Order remained the jealous custodian; by the latter is meant the mission assigned the Order by the Blessed Dominici early in the 15th century. We readily detect the links between Fra Angelico's work and Dominici's doctrines, just as we trace in the latter's writings the ideological premises of a crusade that relied on art as one of its most potent tools of persuasion.

In his exhaustive study of the complex figure of Dominici, Italo Maione pointed out that to acute powers of analysis, a solid grounding in logic and keen missionary zeal, he successfully joined a highly poetic, almost Franciscan feeling for nature. For him the beauties of creation were tangible proof of God's infinite goodness and, in addition to this, an excellent means of striking admiration and enthusiasm into the human soul. He sought in nature a common ground for worldly and mystical experience, and a line of direct communication on the simplest level with his fellow men. He proved himself a subtle and incisive writer, an irresistible speaker, whose words fell naturally into the form of parables and images, which, however, served not merely to drive the example home; much more than that, they were the natural matrix of the concept, of "form" in the Thomist sense of the word, rendering it essentially concrete. Far from decrying learning, Dominici was familiar with the classics and was even something of a Latin stylist. But he taxed the humanists with favoring the classical writers to the detriment of the Scriptures, as if the word of man could surpass the divine logos. Since God-created nature contains a sum of teachings far more salutary than the lucubrations of the philosophers, it is up to us, he maintained, to penetrate nature's secrets. But the end in view being not what is created, but the Creator himself, this knowledge is attainable only through love. "Science without love is not in our image; science is the love that gives us knowledge of ourselves." Love throws light on all things, but finds complete satisfaction in God alone. Making for harmony between the human and the divine, love induces in the soul a state of beatific calm. So as to attain this harmony, love ardently does away with all that is "cold and vain," i.e. the attachment to worldly things, "foolish sensuality." All along the line it roots out and destroys its opposites, i.e. evil.

Only then is nature revealed to us in a state of original purity, in the form in which God created it. If we are to contemplate God, we must scale the ladder of logic from effects to causes, indeed to the prime and unique cause; there, at last, "the thirsty intellect is quenched" and the providential order hitherto admired in the tiniest things of nature broadens out into the universal order of the heavenly hierarchy. "Here are the rejoicing of angels and apostles, the dancing of martyrs and confessors, the choir of virgins, the joys of all the elect. Here are the true sun, the morning star, the flower of the lofty field, the lily of the valley of the just, the rose that never fades, the violet that never withers, carnations, cinnamon and balsam, with the most fragrant perfumes of the Kingdom of the Blessed. Every pleasure has its source in God. There is no pleasure that comes not from Him. How foolish is he who seeks pleasure elsewhere!"

Dominici's description of heavenly delights might describe many a painting by Fra Angelico. Naïvely exclamatory and a little pompous, both are meant to dazzle ingenuous souls with a gorgeous display of images and edify initiates with their symbolism. If this is his model, how deny that, first and foremost, Fra Angelico painted as a preacher preaches. He was too practical a theologian to believe that God could possibly be contemplated as an abstract entity, and the God, saints and angels he paints appeal at once to any man, for they appear as the familiar figures of sensory experience. Only the man who lives spiritually, who loves the world of nature not for itself but for the God who created it, who puts his own experience to good ends, only he can conceive of God in tangible form and perceive His presence in nature. This is the spiritual conduct of life and it incurs both an intellectual and a moral responsibility: intellectual because effects must be traced back to the cause, moral because only then can good be embraced and evil repudiated. The artist proceeds likewise: reverently pursuing his sensory impressions to their purest form, he at last depicts the blissful delights of heaven and, so providing a glimpse of the rewards in store, exhorts the faithful to live holily.

For Cennino Cennini, painting was the art of "eliciting unseen things hidden in the shadow of natural ones... and serving to demonstrate as real the things that are not." For Leon Battista Alberti, on the contrary, "invisible things cannot be said to come within the painter's compass and he only seeks to depict what he sees." Fra Angelico stands midway between these two opposites. For him sensory experience is neither a mere instrument nor an end in itself; it may be brought to perfection, but it cannot be transcended. Aspiring as he does to this "perfect experience," Fra Angelico, of all artists in the first half of the 15th century, is perhaps the one who most explicitly strives to define an ideal of beauty.

We touch, then, on one of the fundamentals of the Thomist aesthetic as practised by Fra Angelico, but it is not the only one. Inveterate churchman that he is, he means to tap the very sources of ontological argument, and a consistent effort to do so is perceptible in the evolution of his painting, especially from about 1433, date of the Linaiuoli Triptych, to 1447, when he first set to work in the Vatican. And since these were the very years in which Alberti was laying the theoretical basis of the new ideas in art, to which he gave a distinctly neo-Platonic bias, it is by no means unreasonable or far-fetched to read a deliberate polemical intent into Fra Angelico's work, or, at the very least, to assume that he strove to contain these new, vigorous currents within the narrow banks of "reformed" scholastic thought, which he hoped to revitalize by drawing on its authentic historical sources.

As was only natural, his warm espousal of the Thomist cause predisposed him to look benignly on those Trecento traditions that Alberti rejected outright, just as his own quest of an ideal of beauty obviously brought him back into the fold of late Trecento aesthetic ideals. But whereas Gothic art took delight in the beauty arising from flawless harmonies of proportion, from the rhythmic continuity of the work as a whole, Fra Angelico fondly expressed his ideal of beauty in each object, each part separately, which contains an intrinsic perfection of its own. The "*debita proportio*" is, to be sure, the fountainhead of beauty, but beauty according to St Thomas Aquinas is "that in which the eye delights." Thus at the same time it is also knowledge; it "satisfies our desire to understand and know." For Fra Angelico beauty is also a lofty value into which art gives us insight; in other words, the concept of the beautiful tends in his mind to merge with the concept of "form," with the embodiment of matter in a "final and perfect thing." The matter at his disposal being pigments, he regards form as the necessary transformation of indistinct matter into distinct and perfect things. The one view he cannot embrace is that of Alberti, who posits form as the image "distinct from all matter" *(ab omni materia separata)*, from which the new conception of space logically followed, space, that is, as a dimension in which things tend to shed their distinctive features and survive only as "values."

Everything points to Fra Angelico's being in touch with the most advanced artists of his day, among whom the handling of space must certainly have been a controversial problem. Obviously he was familiar with the new laws of perspective and did not demur at applying them, though he could scarcely accept them as a geometric system of space representation. Any form of optical empiricism was objectionable to him. From the Thomist point of view no problem of space existed, space being simply the "place" of being or action, while perspective merely provided a means of designating the "perfect place" for "perfect things," or of defining an appropriate hypothetical setting for his pictures, which, never being either quite terrestrial or quite celestial, invariably smack of the hypothetical.

In the Cortona *Annunciation*, for example, the loggia is seen in such trim perspective that it vaguely recalls the architecture of Brunelleschi. What we have is an isometric projection that sets up two planes at right angles to each other, but fails to co-ordinate them. The upshot is two episodes, one enacted *here and now* in the foreground, the other *yonder*, in the background. Why did Fra Angelico avail himself of Brunelleschi's architectural structure, carefully worked out in perspective, arches and columns receding progressively into the distance? Between the two episodes—the Annunciation and Adam and Eve being driven out of the Earthly Paradise—our Thomist painter grasps the obvious connection: the original sin was the cause whose effect became the mission of redemption for which

Christ was born. The recession of the colonnaded portico visually expresses the logical connection of these two events; its value, then, is demonstrative rather than representational.

In *The Coronation of the Virgin* (Louvre) the platform on which the ceremony unfolds is seen in perspective from the base of the steps. And why? Because this was the simplest way of disposing so many figures in strict accordance with celestial hierarchy.

In *The Descent from the Cross* and *The Lamentation over the Dead Christ* (Museo di San Marco, Florence), as in so many predella scenes, he rounded out the main action with far-flung landscape views in impeccable perspective. No wonder, then, that a painter who not only shrinks from regarding space as a geometrical abstraction, but posits it as a "place" peopled with figures, buildings, trees and so on, should be amongst the first to conceive of recession and distance as "landscape." He availed himself of perspective as a means of planting each object in its natural position as a focal point or beacon for the diffusion of light. But the devotional purpose of his pictures being paramount, he sought above all to punctuate the most poignant moments in the divine tragedy. The landscapes come afterwards; when our afflicted gaze has turned away from the painful scene, they soothe the sensibility and induce a mood of pious meditation. They form an integral part of the setting, but above all they lend it an overtone of infinite compassion, subdued exhortation and catharsis. They form, as it were, a bulwark of gentle persuasion, and perhaps a sorrowful, song-like plaint of regret at the blind ingratitude of men, who martyred their own Savior, sent in the name of the Lord who created the beauties of nature.

Weight is lent this view by the fact that in such nearly contemporary frescos as those in the cells at San Marco, the few landscapes we find are stark and terse, purely allusive in nature.

Here his appeal went not to the profane, but to monks. With them he aimed not at inducing compassion and tender emotions, but at suggesting fit themes of meditation. In these scenes, which have all the austere concision of a verse of Scripture, even the "place" is reduced to pure symbol. The same holds good for the Vatican frescos, in which great empty spaces open out to evoke a keen sense of the remote biblical past in which the scenes take place. Here again perspective is frequently brought to bear as a means of separating two successive episodes of the narrative.

But if, with Fra Angelico, space has no objective existence of its own and thus obeys no invariable law, and if perspective becomes merely a convenient way of visualizing the orderly progression of the narrative, light, on the other hand, leads a very real existence and presents a problem that has to be coped with. Both Ghiberti and Cennini acknowledged light as the fundamental on which all vision hinges, but most of their ideas on optics derived from the treatises of Alhazen and Witelo, sources too much tinged with the doctrines of Averroes to be palatable to so orthodox a Christian as Fra Angelico, who indeed took good care not to approach light as he would a mere problem of optics. On the contrary, he held firmly to the Thomist view that light springs not from earthly sources, but emanates from heavenly bodies; that, as such, it has no quantity but is pure quality, and can neither be measured nor propagated. "No one portion of the air illuminates another, but the air as a whole, acted upon by the illuminant, undergoes change" (A. D. Sertillanges, *Saint Thomas d'Aquin*, Alcan, Paris, 1925, vol. I, p. 120). To put it more precisely, light is not propagated in successive waves, as sound is, but leaps from one colored object to another. Variations of intensity arise from the degree to which the light-receiving bodies are diaphanous: "The colored object is such as it is by virtue of gradations in the light, impinging on it according to the extent to which it is diaphanous. For this reason we may say that in bodies themselves colors are *potential*, while it is light that stirs them into *action*" (*op. cit.*, vol. I, p. 119).

Here we have the theoretical ground on which the major premises of Fra Angelico's art are based, the key notion that was shortly to have so decisive an influence on Piero della Francesca: light affects not the "quantity" of colors, modulating them from light to dark, but solely affects their "quality," i.e. it transforms them outright into *other* colors. His conception of light and color plainly evolved, however, in the course of time. Thus in his early work, local colors are quite precisely defined, even though each is lifted to a high level of perfection and purity, while light, in the form of scattered highlights or a profusion of glowing arabesques, adheres to colors like a gossamer film of actual matter, though very different from them in nature. In his middle period light and color tend to merge smoothly, light soaking into color and transforming it. Local colors powdered with light give way to a full-fledged synthesis of color and light, in other words, to "tones." Later still, in the frescos at San Marco, figures and objects have been so disembodied that they live but symbolical lives and no longer offer surfaces congenial to light. The latter, forgoing the splendors of the past, reverts to its pure, imperceptible essence, a bodiless state of diaphaneity no longer dependent on surfaces. It seems more than likely that this sustained effort to fathom the theoretical or metaphysical properties of light arose as a kind of counter-offensive to Alberti's theory or metaphysic of space. Unswerving in his own philosophical convictions, Fra Angelico may well have felt himself duty-bound to discountenance a new concept of space that implicitly rooted every principle of representation in the human mind, to set over against it a concept of light equally theoretical in nature, but such, nevertheless, as not to impair the axiomatic principle that art, like all significant human activities, issues necessarily from God alone.

It plainly follows that if light flows from celestial sources, its presence on earth is providential in character. It is a God-sent boon that reveals nature to our eyes, but it also purifies our sensory experience, shows us created things clad in their original perfection, and restores consummate harmony between the earthly and the celestial. Nature in her perfect state as created by God is only conceivable as being totally luminous. Thus painting—whose noblest task is to refigure the earthly paradise, the Garden of Eden whose existence is vouched for by the Scriptures—must necessarily be the process by which objective "sight" is transformed into light-filled "vision."

His progressive attenuation of light and his firming up of the color texture followed naturally from the assumption that light is a bodiless quality, and that, therefore, it can be transmitted only through a *qualitative* relation between colors. This transmission is essentially direct, "like the stick with which a stone is pushed along." Contours are gradually rounded off, but it would be wrong to interpret this as reflecting—at best very feebly reflecting—the new approach to form such as we find it in the more advanced trends of contemporary painting. If, to an ever-increasing degree, he bulged out contour-lines and converted them into smoothly rhythmic curves, this was no more than an inevitable by-product of his willful efforts to join form and light in satisfactory union.

We are now in a better position to understand why Fra Angelico saw fit to adopt Brunelleschi's perspective, though he could never accept it as a valid theory of space. Impeccably spacing out objects in uniform recession, perspective ensured the even distribution of light and provided against its being deflected or brought up short. We shall see that in Fra Angelico's compositions the specific elements on which perspective hinges —e.g. the walls of buildings—never define the picture space. Sometimes they serve as parallel screens against which figures stand out, and yield either an immediate contrast value or provide the common tonal denominator that links up figures. At other times, in the form of broad planes running athwart the picture, they become light-conductors, shunting it home without ever varying its pitch or dissociating it from color, from the matter, that is, that renders it perceptible to the senses. Fra Angelico could hardly have been blind to the fact that the strict proportions implicit in perspective also served to transform quantity into quality, in other words, to reduce the data of the senses to rational perfection. But he set no store by this, feeling as he did that such truth, issuing from "science without love," differed from the truths that stem from "science with love" to the same extent that even genuine moral wisdom and the new ideals of human dignity differed from saintliness.

*

The notion of *action*, and with it a whole conception of history—this was another point of conflict between the mild "modernism" of Fra Angelico and Alberti's resolute modernity. Regarding action and history as a contest of wills, the latter deduced the principle that action is an end in itself. Ends already attained (i.e. the past) are therefore legitimate and justified. As against this, action has no window on the future or on the ultimate destiny of the soul; it clinches and seals, but its horizons fail to transcend the here-and-now, just as the painter who records only what he sees can only depict what has happened, or may be imagined to happen.

Fra Angelico, too, ventured to locate and interpret action, but action devoid of any clash of will or personality. How indeed can the necessity to act be denied, without abjuring the doctrine of free will? But Christ having redeemed mankind, men on the whole, whatever their failings or lapses, must in the end choose the good; thus the outcome of action is secured, conflicts and suspense availing nothing. Action as conceived by Fra Angelico can have nothing in common then with the "inventions" of Alberti, its evolution being foreseen and foreordained: the prefect who adjures the saint to sacrifice to alien gods is wasting his breath, and the martyrdom that follows is not a tragic *dénouement* but the solemn fulfillment of an act whereby the saint enters on the glories of eternal life. The prefect himself is but the midwife of Providence, speeding the saint on his way to beatitude, and no one takes his cruelties seriously. In the proper sense of the term, he is an actor aware of his role and intent on living up to it. All this accounts for the patently theatrical character of Fra Angelico's predella pictures; they are like scenes of miracle plays. He makes no attempt to give the illusion of events taking place before our very eyes, but simply narrates episodes from the history of the Church.

Yet Fra Angelico cannot be described as a narrator in the sense that Gentile da Fabriano had been before him and Benozzo Gozzoli after him. Properly speaking, he is a preacher fond of digressing from exhortation to example, but one who never relaxes the taut didactic threads that sustain his sermon. For him what he paints are so many "examples," which he skillfully varies in keeping with the point he hopes to put across. In most of his predella scenes, Fra Angelico—like Dominici in his *Lucula Noctis*—made a show of the monkish ingenuity of the strict Observant who sees no use or profit in re-examining the facts of history, as the first humanists then were doing. After all, he seems to say, what is history if not the record of events long past, but always willed and shaped by God? If we choose to recount some of them, this is because they exemplify commendable deeds and good lives. All that is asked of the spectator is an edified and guileless admiration such as that produced by the passion plays at Eastertime. To this end, all the figures must be comely and prepossessing; where this is out of the question, they must give the impression of being disguised or deformed. The landscape or "natural setting," too, must be attractive and pleasant, since the event lies within the order of nature rather than history. It will be the more convincing the more it seems miraculous, since God manifests his will through miracles and all nature is a miracle.

But when the artist paints for his fellow monks at San Marco and invites them not to admire but to meditate, his landscapes are divested of their smiling colors and figures are no longer linked by the narrative action. The reference to history, however, now strikes so much deeper than elsewhere that figures are reduced to mere symbols, signal forms of thought long ruminated over. Out of this conscience-stricken juncture soon arose the Vatican frescos, with their lofty moral tenor and their solemn, "official" version of history. These scenes are a crystal-clear exposition of religious humanism, bent as they are on resurrecting the early Christians with the same moral fervor the humanists put into reviving ancient Rome. Fra Angelico was now an honored and influential spokesman of all that the Curia Romana stood for. And just as in his intercourse with the great of the Church he abandoned the "sweet vernacular" for polished Latin, so he henceforth fell back on themes drawn exclusively from the miracle-filled lives of the earliest defenders of the faith.

If we are to grasp the nature of action in his work, we perhaps do best to examine it in the light of what Lanzi called his *giottismo*. Obviously Fra Angelico cannot be lumped together with the crowd of traditional-minded painters who, even as late as the mid-15th century, prided themselves on descending from Giotto by way of his direct followers. Instead of "descending" from him, Fra Angelico "rejoins" Giotto on the latter's own ground without crossing the shaky bridges of a stultified tradition. He "rejoined" him in much the same way, at roughly the same time, and in much the same circumstances, that the enlightened minds of the 15th century were harking back to Dante. He gave a new lease of life to the best in Giotto, and he went about this with the thoroughness of a purist (see, for example, the *Lamentation over the Dead Christ* at San Marco). Lanzi had detected the "imprint of Giotto" in the "posing of the figures and the balance of this art"—in other words, in his manner of setting forth the action. Fra Angelico could accept neither Alberti's penchant for submerging action into history, nor the loose and casual narrative of Masolino, nor the half courtly, half biblical tone of Ghiberti. He was enough of a humanist to face the fact that, after the scientific approach of Brunelleschi and Alberti, after Donatello's forthright realism, even earlier, in fact, in the latter half of the Trecento, with the quest of purely formal abstractions, art had shaken off the cloak of religion and no longer ministered to didactic and moral ends exclusively. He saw no other remedy to this but a return to the fundamentals of a vital religious art such as he found them in Giotto. And back to Giotto he went, as Lanzi phrased it, in "the posing of his figures and the balance" of his art. Which is to say that he sacrificed both the tension of Late Gothic and the new dramatizing of action for equanimity and compositional harmony. Very possibly he glimpsed the striking parallel between Giotto's masterful handling of architecture, not yet crystallized into an abstract geometry of space, but built up entirely on the *ethos* of history, and the four-square, realistic-minded architecture of the philosophical system erected by St Thomas Aquinas. Like Dante, Giotto seemed to him an incarnation of Thomist thought. The very humanity of Giotto's figures must have seemed in his eyes, first, to embody the idea of God as nobly as earthly beings can embody it, and secondly, to extol the moral life as the bastion of Godhead in this world. It is strange to say, but had Giotto asserted himself in scientific rather than moral terms, he might have opened the way to outright pantheism, the one solution to which Fra Angelico was perhaps irreconcilably opposed.

We cannot help feeling that Giotto's deep moral sense largely accounts for his contained power, his sublime gravity of composition, his unbroken lines and muted colors. Here, very probably, we have the origin of Fra Angelico's color, the example that led him progressively to abandon the precious enamel-like tints and heavy chiaroscuro bequeathed him by Late Gothic. Very probably, too, he owed his rediscovery of Giotto to Masaccio. The full effects of his *neo-giottismo*, however, are only felt in the works of his maturity, being the logical outcome of long meditation. One reason more, perhaps, for seeing in it a deliberately one-sided interpretation of Masaccio's art, whose shadow loomed ever larger in his late works—but an increasingly moral shadow rather than an aesthetic one.

If this is so, we go wrong in viewing Fra Angelico's position amid the cross-currents of Quattrocento art trends as one of frank compromise; it is rather that of a mediator fully aware of his role. Between the formalism of late Trecento traditions and the new theories of Alberti, he interposed what might be described as "religious naturalism." The new theories of space structure offered him a ready means of reconstituting the real world. But the world is God's handiwork, and since the excellence of art lies in its power to render forms in all their pristine purity, it can only arise in terms of natural things. The process of art is the same as that which strips reality of man's "vanities and foulness"; it is both a moral and an intellectual process.

As we delve into the nature of Fra Angelico's ideal of beauty, we soon realize that it does not depend on any predetermined norms of proportion or balance. Each line in itself is vigilantly carried to an extreme of flawless purity that quite frees it from the pull of the senses. In his hands this becomes a kind of inward sifting and filtering of images, leaving only what is "intrinsically desirable" and thereby awakening an echo in the loftiest of human faculties: the desire for good. We cannot help ourselves, but are bound to name and describe God in all-too-human terms; even our idea of His infinity depends on what we perceive in the natural world. It thus seemed to him that the only worth-while "naturalism" in any art, as an inquiry into the "truth" of nature, consists in the choice of the purest terms and the most perfect things, and that art is therefore necessarily religious.

Yet even his naturalism bore a strain of allegory. In the first place, his fusion of the natural and the allegorical is one of the salient features of the reform which, on the strength of the new aesthetic ideas, he hoped to bring about in religious painting properly so called. The very idea of divinity implies an allegorical interpretation; God having no definable form, He can only be represented in terms of some analogy with natural forms. But the narration of the lives of the saints too is inevitably allegorical, since these are of interest not so much as historical events, but as moments in time favorable to the manifestation of "saintliness." With Fra Angelico, as in the writings of Dominici, landscape and the natural world are consistently allegorical: architecture, flowers and meadows, quiet orchards, sharp rocks and so on. Flowers are always those of the "lofty field"; their fragrance is the "balm" of sainthood, gardens are glimpses of paradise, light is a ray of the morning star, rocks allude to the stony path of earthly life, and landscapes signify how miraculous nature is and how natural miracles are. His allegory could not exist apart from nature, his ideas being channeled into the tangible stuff that gave them form or sublimated them into the impalpable substance that is light. This, after all, was but a way of suspending the things he painted between heaven and earth, a way of idealizing what is natural and materializing the supernatural (Longhi calls this the "supernaturalism" of Fra Angelico). In other words, his allegory is both naturalistic and theological; it implies rapture since contemplation precedes the act of painting, and implies prayer since the act of painting broadcasts what prayer entreats. True rapture, it might he added, arises only out of communion and predication, preferably within the silent walls of the monastery, otherwise within the broader circle of the faithful, but always within the community, the *ecclesia*.

This is *docta pietas*, and as such inseparable from rhetoric, which is the expression of the Christian spirit as opposed to the materialism of Averroes (described by Petrarch as *mercenarius et infamis artifex*). In the light of *docta pietas*, the new theories of art—i.e. the quest of a guiding principle, a law of nature— opened the rejoicing prospect of a spiritual renewal. A common front rose up against lifeless traditions, which were perpetuated by mere technical recipes and the coldest formalism—a front on the whole bravely liberal. Room was still left for divergent views within the movement, however, and among the learned and the theoretical-minded arose discussions of principle bearing on the nature of being, the moral life and destiny of man, the interpretation of sapiential texts.

This was the Florentine art world of the 15th century. In it Fra Angelico stood for the aesthetic of St Thomas Aquinas as against the Neo-Platonism of Leon Battista Alberti. But he also stood for the possibility of dialectical exchange between the two. Between the historical realism of Donatello and Alberti's challenging theories of history, Fra Angelico set up an intermediate "naturalism," thus pointing the way to an art that was no longer motionless "representation," but a lively human colloquy. He pointed the way to the great story-tellers of the

15th century, from Benozzo Gozzoli to Ghirlandaio. In addition to this, Fra Angelico posited light as the qualitative principle by which human experience, limited in scope and heavy with "quantity," might be sublimated into a supreme ideal of being. This was the point of departure from which Piero della Francesca achieved his great synthesis of light and space, welding together the complementary aspirations of 15th-century painters: insight into both the human and divine sides of the world, and form that expressed both the dramatic contrasts of man's history and the eternal, rational laws of nature.

THE VIRGIN AND CHILD ENTHRONED WITH ANGELS BETWEEN STS DOMINIC,
NICHOLAS OF BARI, JOHN THE BAPTIST AND CATHERINE OF ALEXANDRIA,
DETAIL, CENTRAL PANEL. 1437. GALLERIA NAZIONALE DELL'UMBRIA, PERUGIA.

WORKS

I

ALTARPIECES AND PREDELLA SCENES

ALTARPIECES AND PREDELLA SCENES

A LONG-STANDING tradition describes Fra Angelico as a pupil of Gherardo Starnina, a belated follower of Giotto who died in 1413. This permits us to suppose that, very possibly, he was already painting and illuminating by the time he entered on his noviciate in 1407. Evidence of such activity has been read into the *Diurnus Dominicalis*, a set of early 15th-century miniatures in the Biblioteca Laurenziana, Florence, whose style presents obvious affinities with that of Fra Angelico's first known works (this interesting point is covered by A.M. Ciaranfi, in *L'Arte*, 1932). Actually the history of his painting and the study of his style cannot begin before 1418, when the brotherhood of Observant Dominicans to which he belonged returned to Fiesole from ten years of exile at Cortona. Only then did he come steadily into contact with Florentine art life, which must have provided the stimulation his slowly maturing powers had hitherto lacked.

The decade from 1420 to 1430 was an eventful one for Florentine art: Brunelleschi built his great dome for the cathedral of Santa Maria del Fiore, Donatello produced much of his finest sculpture, and Masaccio inaugurated what Vasari called the "modern" style with his frescos in the Brancacci Chapel at Santa Maria del Carmine. Among the secondary factors that hastened the rise of this new art was the arrival in Florence of Gentile da Fabriano in about 1422. He stayed just long enough to paint an *Adoration of the Magi* (1423) for the church of Santa Trinità, now in the Uffizi. But he brought with him from the North that "keen sense of naturalistic detail" (Longhi), whose vigorous repercussions proved that, for all its charms and refinement, the late Trecento tradition of Florentine painting had worked itself out at last and come to a standstill in a mire of conventional formulae.

THE ANNUNCIATION. CA. 1430. $(62\frac{3}{4} \times 70\frac{3}{4}")$
MUSEO DEL GESÙ, CORTONA.

Longhi has tentatively assigned to the years 1425-1430 a small group of pictures by Fra Angelico, all of them significant works. Though the imprint of Masaccio is unmistakable, they also display an observational shrewdness and a certain finesse in the brushwork that can only stem from Gentile da Fabriano (Roberto Longhi, *Critica d'Arte*, 1941, p. 173). At least three

THE ANNUNCIATION.
DETAIL: ADAM AND EVE CAST OUT OF PARADISE.
MUSEO DEL GESÙ, CORTONA.

points tell heavily in favor of taking these as the initial step, still timid as yet, in his career as a painter. Most important of all, any number of inconspicuous clues seem to betray the illuminator's hand: the lay-out, the skill with which figures are arranged within a limited picture space, and the way colors are laid on and clot, as it were. Next, these works break radically with the outright linearism of Lorenzo Monaco and, without presuming to put across any theory, they run counter to the traditions of the day. Lastly, they reveal not only a first-hand knowledge of Masaccio and a warm sympathy for his structural sobriety and concision, but also a very tepid interest in the moral and theoretical premises inherent in Masaccio's art. It would take a stretch of the imagination to say that, in this early group of works, Fra Angelico showed any doctrinarian concern with problems of space and space representation, then a matter of heated debate. Yet the sharpness of his images against a picture space that had hitherto swum in vagueness, his foreshortenings, diffident but closely knit, the relative starkness of his forms, his colors welling up against the contours that bind them, his light that falls like dew over objects—all this confers on these works a weight and consistence that were completely new.

A case in point is *The Virgin and Child enthroned with Twelve Angels* (Staedelsches Institut, Frankfort). The choir formed by the angels is more like a chain than a garland; they form a ring whose tautness and density are unexampled in any work by Ghiberti. Seen in a variety of foreshortenings, figures stand quite apart from one another. They fail to set up a rhythmic cadence, but each is linked to the center like a spoke to the hub of a wheel. As against this, imprisoned in the strict perspective of the tabernacle, alone in a large empty space, are the Virgin and Child. Should we be tempted to compare this notion of space with that embodied in some particular piece of architecture by Brunelleschi, the first great master of perspective, our comparison would bear on the circular perspective centering on the lantern atop the dome of Santa Maria del Fiore rather than the longitudinal vistas that characterize such churches as San Lorenzo and Santo Spirito. Though more tightly knit and more developed plastically, the same lay-out occurs in the central group of the altarpiece in the church of San Domenico at Fiesole (this work was extensively restored about 1501 by Lorenzo di Credi, who, among other liberties, took that of painting out the gold ground, which he replaced with an architectural setting of arcades that open out on to a landscape). Here the angels form a tightly drawn circle out of which the central, dominant figure of the Virgin rises. A host of similarities with the *Virgin and St Anne*, jointly painted by Masaccio and Masolino, come to mind at once. Note how the eye-balls, the slightly curving mouth and the straight-bridged nose fit snugly into the oval of the face, as into a geometrical design.

Yet, even though he branched out in the direction of the new art, Fra Angelico showed little or no interest in defining space for the containment of well-modeled volumes. Instead he seemed intent on expressing an ideal of beauty, one very different, needless to say, from the courtly ideal of Late Gothic, based nevertheless on the intrinsic qualities or perfection of things in themselves and not on their spatial value. He had no prejudice against a "desirable" or "attractive" ideal of beauty, but he realized that everything that exists aspires to a degree of perfection which, in reality, is its true nature, its original, divinely ordained form. While Masaccio boldly asserted his power to people space with solid bodies and crowned them with the massive figure of the Virgin, Fra Angelico piously went his own way. He painted the steps of her tabernacle in sloping perspective, seated her on the edge of the throne, and deprived her of all physical weight by surrounding her with a

THE MARRIAGE OF THE VIRGIN, DETAIL.
SCENE FROM THE PREDELLA OF THE ANNUNCIATION.
MUSEO DEL GESÙ, CORTONA.

radiant choir of angels, while the folds of her mantle float weightlessly round her body. As we study the two pairs of Dominican fathers flanking the throne, we marvel at the precision with which the head of each fits into the circle of his cowl, and the minute care that went into planting each figure squarely on the tiled floor. But we note, too, that his chief interest bore perhaps on the alternating sequence of white tunics and dark cloaks. In the San Domenico altarpiece he clung to flat colors and relied on sinuous contours, as they wend their way amid contrasting values, to secure a unified scheme of flat planes that precludes the use of chiaroscuro.

His quest of an inner source of light inseparable from forms and colors—colors no longer being "effect" but "cause"— shows through in such bright gold backgrounds as we find in the *Madonna della Stella*, also in the ground of mingled gold and color of *The Annunciation and The Adoration*, both reliquary panels from Santa Maria Novella and now in the Museo di San Marco, which lend themselves to a whole range of color intensity and vibration. If we are to believe the *Chronica* of Biliotti of 1570-1600, these works date from 1430 at the latest and may even be earlier. If so, they prove that even then he was making a serious attempt to render space through light.

The most significant work of this early period is the Cortona *Annunciation*. Painted shortly after 1430, it is the prototype of a host of variants either by Fra Angelico himself or his pupils. We have already referred to the symbolic perspective of the loggia, the first sign of the artist's doctrinarian preoccupations. But the loggia also fills a purely formal function, being the "standard," the "modulus," on which the composition turns. The two main arches curving over Mary and the archangel Gabriel are swung down heavily enough to inhibit the impression of depth, while on the left the swift recession of foreshortened columns constricts the arches to the utmost. And since the loggia is obviously intended to frame the figures, not to create space, we see that by thus juggling broad and narrow archways the painter succeeded in building up the entire scene on a ground-plan of broad and narrow curves. Mary's mantle, as it flows down her back, echoes the camber of the foreshortened arches, while the angel, who is a bundle of curves, echoes the frontal arches. The result is that the angel, glimpsed in the very act of alighting, betrays no movement at all, so precisely is he inscribed in his colonnaded frame, whereas every line in the Virgin's figure is galvanized and taut, as she starts from her absorption in the prayer book on her knee.

THE VISITATION. SCENE FROM THE PREDELLA OF THE ANNUNCIATION. MUSEO DEL GESÙ, CORTONA.

Ang. 7

THE VISITATION, DETAIL. SCENE FROM THE PREDELLA OF THE ANNUNCIATION.
MUSEO DEL GESÙ, CORTONA.

Ang. 9

THE VISITATION, DETAIL. SCENE FROM THE PREDELLA OF THE ANNUNCIATION.
MUSEO DEL GESÙ, CORTONA.

The supple curves of this composition are part and parcel of an ideal of beauty, a principle of harmony. The fact remains, however, that they entirely subserve the perspective of the loggia, which determines the "ideal setting" of the scene and governs the even distribution of light. Granted that we see things by virtue of their colors; it is still light that enables color to rise from a *potential* to an *actual* state, from "quantity" to "quality." These curves not only delimit color zones of various size, but also govern the relationship between colors, and this in terms of the ideal place where light is evenly shed. These are the lines that lift all colors to the same level of quality, to the same pitch of luminous intensity. Proof that with Fra Angelico all space is conceived as light, and light as the supreme quality revealed in the form of things, is furnished by the column rising between the Virgin and the angel, whose task is to provide a break, a pause, a caesura of light. It foreshadows the famous column we find in many works by Piero della Francesca. And like Piero's, it has its origin in Brunelleschi's conception of the column as the basic form of all buildings. Further proof lies in the palm-tree, whose trunk falls into line with the colonnade, and whose stylized leaves echo and greatly multiply the rhythm of the arches. This tree binds the architecture to the landscape, the setting of the main episode to that of the secondary episode.

In the predella scenes, too, perspective is invariably enlisted as a physical vehicle of celestial light; it provides the key to the entire register of pictorial values. And since the place itself is bound up with the scene being enacted, perspective also serves to sustain the narrative. It adjusts recession according as figure-groups are scattered or thickly sown; it specifies the train of events, dividing them off and linking them up at the same time; it staggers a variety of plane surfaces that serve as screens reflecting a beamless, bodiless light in all directions.

THE ADORATION OF THE MAGI.
SCENE FROM THE PREDELLA OF THE ANNUNCIATION.
MUSEO DEL GESÙ, CORTONA.

Of all the scenes on the predella of the Cortona *Annunciation*, one in particular, *The Visitation*, has attracted the attention of critics. It is only half a century since Douglas and Berenson pointed out that here, for the first time, we have the picture of an actual landscape: Lake Trasimene, near Perugia, seen from the hill of Cortona. Mario Salmi (*Arti Figurative*, 1947, pp. 82-83) goes even further. Assuming Piero della Francesca to have been Fra Angelico's pupil, he hazards the guess that this extraordinary scene may well be by Piero, the pupil having resolved to show the master the difference between actual daylight and an abstract, theological kind of light. The scene differs so distinctly from the others that such an hypothesis is by no means far-fetched. Unfortunately, for it to be plausible, the work would have to date from after 1435, several years after the Linaiuoli Triptych, which is inadmissible. What is more, the episodic progression of the predella scenes is orderly and methodical in the extreme; the remote horizon beyond Lake Trasimene even has its counterpart in the deeply receding perspective of the nave in *The Presentation in the Temple*. Occurring at regular intervals, these two vistas break up and relieve the three other scenes, which are broader and shallower. Why should we grow suspicious at a deliberate contrast between daylight and perspective-guided lighting? His aim was not an abstract, but a "natural" rendering of godhead. The whole predella, furthermore, proclaims itself to be an analysis of light's relation to perspective. It is not by chance that the first of the three large scenes, *The Marriage of the Virgin*, is located in normal architectural perspective, whereas the second, an *Adoration of the Magi*, stands against a skew background in which buildings alternate with landscape, while the third, *The Death of the Virgin*, looms up against a flat ground of bare rocks running parallel to the figures. No wonder, then, that *The Visitation* takes place in a picture space replete with light, and *The Presentation* in the semi-darkness of an architectural interior seen in perspective. This contrast between architecture and nature, theoretical perspective and natural perspective, is one of the earliest examples of its kind in painting, dating from shortly after 1430.

By then Masaccio had already showed what a painter could do with the theories of space and perspective that Brunelleschi had put forward and applied in architecture. But Masaccio's interpretation seemed to postulate, even for painting, a principle of monumentality, a notion of structure inherent in form, that precluded any venture into naturalistic landscape.

To reinstate the latter, it was not enough simply to extend the logic of Brunelleschi's initial theories. What was wanted was a kind of dogmatic necessity such as Fra Angelico alone could bring to bear. God, he felt, had created not space, but the things that fill space, and the light by which we see them. Perspective, then, is no more than a means—and an "intellectual" means—of visualizing things, of appreciating God's creation in its infinite variety and the constancy of its laws. In an anonymous *Life of Brunelleschi* written in the 15th century, the author dwells at length on the fact that painters apply his

THE PRESENTATION IN THE TEMPLE.
SCENE FROM THE PREDELLA OF THE ANNUNCIATION.
MUSEO DEL GESÙ, CORTONA.

Ang. 11

building proportions to landscape and draw on his rules of architecture in painting "houses, plains, mountains and landscapes of sundry kinds." There is no doubt in my mind that Fra Angelico was the first to carry over architectural perspective into the realm of the naturalistic landscape. He was too shrewd a churchman to decry a principle of differentiated creation simply because it implied an unorthodox conception of space. But his was also too cultured a mind not to see that this conception of space promised to be a highly useful tool in the study of nature. We may therefore assume that, in the predella of the Cortona altarpiece, he deliberately made the very first attempt to apply perspective to natural scenery, the earliest example in painting of naturalism based on theoretical principles.

★

The Linaiuoli Triptych is the first work by Fra Angelico whose date is known for certain; records prove it to have been commissioned in 1433 for the guild-hall of the Florentine flax-makers *(linaiuoli)*. This altarpiece vouches for the influence of Lorenzo Ghiberti, ten years his senior, who designed the marble frame into which the triptych is set, and which is structurally in keeping with the bevel-edged border of angel musicians. It vouches, too, for the inevitable links between Fra Angelico and humanism and gives us our first glimpse of those literary leanings that henceforth colored his entire output. This altarpiece introduced a new type of "Virgin in glory," solemn and intensely human at once, and a new veneration voiced in accents of an almost classical eloquence. Isolated within narrow bounds of space, a little cramped by heavy, overhanging curtains, the Virgin is distinctly statuesque; such, too, is the

◀ THE LINAIUOLI TRIPTYCH, CENTRAL PANEL. AFTER 1433. (129½ × 102″) MUSEO DI SAN MARCO, FLORENCE.

THE ADORATION OF THE MAGI. PREDELLA SCENE FROM THE LINAIUOLI
TRIPTYCH. MUSEO DI SAN MARCO, FLORENCE.

impression made by the large figures of saints painted on the
front and back of the wings. By "statuesque" no allusion to
relief or modeling is intended. I refer simply to the humanist
conception of the statue, which led Alberti to entitle his treatise
on sculpture *De Statua*. According to this conception, the aim
of the work of art was not to "represent" but to "celebrate,"
not to picture the physical man, but the historical figure. The
statue was "history" devoid of episodes or events, a tangible
expression of the eulogy or sermon.

And much as in a sermon, what matters in a painting by Fra Angelico is the elocution, the noble strain of language, the purity and continuity of form—rhetoric, in other words. The very rhetoric regarded by Petrarch as our most precious heritage from classical Antiquity, as the appropriate character assumed by every activity of the human mind, for it is the art of using language so as to persuade or influence others. The object in view was not to see or represent, but to admire and rouse admiration. The "admirable" henceforth became the

THE MARTYRDOM OF ST MARK. PREDELLA SCENE FROM THE
LINAIUOLI TRIPTYCH. MUSEO DI SAN MARCO, FLORENCE.

leading theme of Fra Angelico's painting, at least of the works he intended for those who live in the world and require spiritual guidance in the accomplishment of their daily tasks.

What is undeniable is that, at least in part, this ideal of human dignity stemmed from Masaccio. Fra Angelico realized, however, that if he was to exhort and persuade, and not merely to inspire awe, he had in a sense to transcend Masaccio's rugged and salient forms. For this he looked to Ghiberti and found what he wanted in the latter's sculpture and relief-work: forms rhythmic and ornate, yet austere in their "rhetoric," woven into a profusion of themes and motifs with consummate elegance of expression and elocution.

This does not mean that Fra Angelico sought to mingle alien elements with his religious motifs so as to gratify the powerful group of cloth merchants who had commissioned the altarpiece. Yet a latent interest in "history" underlies the work, which even succeeds in adding something to the humanist ideal of man's dignity. As for perspective, so for history: provided it was not set up as a supreme and exclusive end in itself, or as the sole source of knowledge or the sole reliable guide, Fra Angelico had no dogmatic objection to it in principle. God Himself saw fit to assume the form of man and endure the vicissitudes of earthly life. Therefore, provided it is religious and not profane, history can guide us in the ways of God and impart a lofty didactic message. And here Fra Angelico dwells so heavily on this didactic role that, when all is said and done, the mystical theme has been thrust largely into the background. The angel musicians of the frame strike us as no more than "poor small souls," graceful but trivial, when we compare them with the resolute humanity of the Virgin and saints, and with the events that unfold in the three predella scenes.

It is significant that in this predella no vestige remains of the *perspectiva naturalis* that prevails in the predella of the

THE NAMING OF JOHN THE BAPTIST.
BEFORE 1435. $(10\frac{1}{4} \times 9\frac{3}{8}'')$
MUSEO DI SAN MARCO, FLORENCE.

Cortona *Annunciation*. The buildings are but the historical landmarks of the spot in which the scenes are enacted. History not being an end in itself, however, and the pictured events therefore assuming an apologetic value, the painter deems it sufficient simply to show that they occur at a remote time and place. It has recently been suggested (Pierre Francastel, *Peinture et Société*, 1951, p. 21) that Fra Angelico's manner of locating and presenting an event may owe something to the theater. There is, in fact, much to be said for this view. The edifying episodes of his predella scenes are not only like a pictorial version of sermons or prayer, but smack distinctly of the miracle play. Even backdrops, shown in scrupulous perspective, have the generalized, functional character of stage sets; they share intimately in the action and echo the movement of the figures. According to Thomist doctrine, movement is simply change of place, and continual changes of backdrop quite successfully suggest such movement. In *St Peter preaching*, the architectural "sets" fold and unfold like the tall panels of a draft-screen flexing on their hinges, and forthwith tie up the action of the different figure-groups. In *The Martyrdom of St Mark*, a peculiar perspective effect of slanting planes is thrown up behind the terror-stricken executioners as they scurry away. Most theatrical of all is the freakish hailstorm that beats about the ears of these hapless "villains," while the "good souls" a few feet away bask in the serene light of a cloudless sky.

But this is not all. In juggling and combining perspective (or architecture) and light (or nature), Fra Angelico continually brings perspective screens of this kind into play, so as to set up a suitable relationship between what might be called the "generic place" and the "specific place," in other words between open, boundless space and the earthbound scene of the narrative. Two small panels illustrate this: *St James the Great freeing Hermogenes* (Collection of the Duc des Cars, Paris) and

The Naming of John the Baptist (Museo di San Marco, Florence).
In the first, behind a figure-group, we glimpse a loggia receding
in perspective; in the second, what seems to be a corridor, also
dropping away in perspective. Yet in each case the vista in recession has no other function than that of linking the closed space
of the main episode to the open horizons beyond; there light
caresses the softly curving flanks of hills, gleams on the leaves
of trees and pours a crystalline sheen over distant houses, while
in the foreground, where the action is taking place, light
blends into the colors, enhances their purity and sets up between
them those relations of quality we call "tone."

★

From 1435 to about 1440, Fra Angelico painted a whole
series of altarpieces around the traditional theme and lay-out of
the Virgin surrounded by saints. In the first, in the church
of San Domenico at Cortona, the Virgin enthroned occupies
the center, flanked on one side by St Mark and St John the
Baptist, on the other by St John the Evangelist and Mary
Magdalen. The work has much in common with the Linaiuoli
Triptych, though striking a more modest and retiring note
on the whole and more conventional in its grace. Having by
then made a thoroughgoing study of Ghiberti's relief-work, he
realized the extent to which a traditional foundation underlay
its veneer of humanism.

A second altarpiece, painted for the church of San Domenico
at Perugia (now in the Galleria Nazionale, Perugia), marked
a fresh rallying of his powers. Records prove it to date from
1437. Still wholly Gothic, the frame divides the work symme-
trically into three bays. In the center sits a wistful Virgin with
angels bringing up the rear; on the left are St Dominic and
St Nicholas, on the right St John the Baptist and St Catherine
of Alexandria, while in the tondi above the lateral panels

are the angel Gabriel and the Virgin Annunciate. From now on his perspective smoothly functioned as a formal principle independent of visual experience. It is applied so rigorously to the throne that it frames the Virgin in an abstract, light-filled geometric design, while the angels shyly sidling behind her form a secondary niche whence their radiant colors stand out against the gold ground. The tondi are set into the frame with the same accuracy of perspective as the circular windows in Brunelleschi's buildings.

By the time this altarpiece was painted, the new trends in art had been defined, though from one angle only, by Leon Battista Alberti in his treatise on painting. Fra Angelico, then, may well have deliberately set out to voice his own views (which were those of the Church) with respect to humanist tendencies. Whether acquainted or not with Alberti's writings, he could scarcely have failed to see that the new theories of vision fast gaining ground were bound to secularize art, to "bring it down to earth" in ways to which Alberti was already calling attention. The opposing arguments were clear: Alberti advocated an art dealing solely with visible things, while Cennini had stated the case for a "loftier" mission, that of revealing things unseen. Fra Angelico could embrace neither thesis, since for him, though he held God to be knowable only through nature, an intellectual process was still necessary to attain this knowledge. Perspective, then, was acceptable as an intellectual process, but not as an absolute system of space. He therefore chose a middle way in his peculiar use of perspective: fixing his precise standpoint, he laid out every element with scrupulous symmetry, drew in forms with faultless geometrical

◀ ST DOMINIC. DETAIL FROM THE VIRGIN AND CHILD ENTHRONED WITH ANGELS
BETWEEN STS DOMINIC, NICHOLAS OF BARI, JOHN THE BAPTIST AND CATHERINE
OF ALEXANDRIA. 1437. GALLERIA NAZIONALE DELL'UMBRIA, PERUGIA.

regularity, and stepped up colors to their maximum luminous
intensity, so as to stress the status of light as cause and not
effect. Light thus assumed with him much the same abstract
conceptual value as did space in the new theories; from space
and light he shifted the emphasis to form and light. For him
perfect form, perfectly expressing both a scientific and a religious
ideal, was that which becomes one with absolute light, that
which cancels out "effect" and fully reinstitutes light's primary
quality, that of "cause."

As far as form and color go, the key to the Perugia altarpiece lies in the three small vases of flowers in front of the
Virgin. Located beyond the point where the perspective takes
effect, they stand on a strip of spotted marble that sets up a

ST NICHOLAS ADDRESSING AN IMPERIAL EMISSARY AND ST NICHOLAS
SAVING A SHIP AT SEA. PREDELLA SCENE FROM THE PERUGIA ALTARPIECE.
1437. (13 × 24¾″) PINACOTECA VATICANA.

kind of neutral zone of indeterminate space. These vases are
delineated with such clarity and conviction, with so obvious an
intent to create perfect, self-sufficient things, that they immediately bring Van Eyck to mind. They are meant to demonstrate
that natural form, stainless, free of accidental tares, reduced to
its pristine purity, coincides with symbolic form. Each rose
becomes a *rosa mystica*. Perspective restores the base of the
throne to its truest, most spontaneous natural form and, as
we lift our gaze, we grasp in its entirety a new conception of
form, born of perfect identity between color and light. The
blue mass of the Virgin's robe, for example, rises up in front
of the throne in soft folds and eminences, molded by juxtaposed
planes, until it takes its rightful place in the luminous cavity

59

of the niche between the four angels. Hands, bodies and faces
are modeled in sheer translucency, and only fleeting accents and
silvery, transparent scumbles mark the regular curving of planes.

On the predella are *Scenes from the Life of St Nicholas of Bari*
(two belong to the Pinacoteca Vaticana, one to the Galleria

THE UNLOADING OF THE WHEAT. DETAIL FROM ST NICHOLAS
ADDRESSING AN IMPERIAL EMISSARY. PREDELLA SCENE FROM THE PERUGIA
ALTARPIECE. 1437. PINACOTECA VATICANA.

Nazionale, Perugia). Seeking something of an antidote perhaps to the new notions of "invention" and "history," Fra Angelico reverted again to his favorite store of themes, *The Golden Legend* of Jacopo Voragine, whose naïve and complaisant stream of narrative he echoed. The scenes are somewhat less theatrical than those on the predella of the Linaiuoli Triptych. The relation of perspective to light having been settled, there was no need now for "stage sets." All nature becomes a miraculous setting in which miraculous events quite naturally occur. Thus it is that we find no more than a very queer crest of crooked rocks separating the two different times and places in the episodes of *St Nicholas addressing an Imperial Emissary* and *St Nicholas saving a Ship at Sea*. On the one hand is the quiet inlet with ships riding at anchor; on the other, a dark storm unleashing its fury and the ship wallowing in the troughs of a heavy sea. In the second picture, too, a single plane receding in perspective separates the two episodes of *St Nicholas saving Three Men condemned to Death* and *The Death of St Nicholas*. But this plane serves to demonstrate that light and form can as readily be fused in an open landscape as in a closed space.

Another altarpiece, from the Dominican convent of San Vincenzo di Annalena, shows *The Virgin and Child enthroned with Sts Peter Martyr, Cosmas, Damian, John the Evangelist, Lawrence and Francis*. Stretching across the background are the austere façade of an arcaded building and a precious tapestry hanging. The Virgin presides from a marble throne before a conch-like niche; on either side, like outspread wings, stand the saints. Here, instead of a "Virgin in glory," we have a *sacra conversazione*. The saints are admitted to the same ground as the Virgin and bathe in the same light. This, however, emanates from her person, for she is still the center, the perfect form in which light retains intact its supernatural qualities. The conch-like design above her head secures an even distribution of light

Ang. 20

THE CORONATION OF THE VIRGIN.
CA. 1430-1440. $(82\frac{3}{4} \times 83\frac{1}{2}'')$
LOUVRE, PARIS.

around her; the geometrical regularity of the grooves and fluting serves to warrant this distribution both from the rational and the naturalistic points of view. Colors have grown more translucent still, and softly falling shadows, instead of attenuating light, simply shunt it in another direction; glancing off invisible planes, it assumes shape in immaterial form.

In these same years Piero della Francesca was working alongside Domenico Veneziano at Florence. We can readily imagine the impression made on him by this miraculous balance of forms and light, which so plainly affected the course of his art. Alberti had created a metaphysic of space out of neo-Platonic data. Similarly, Fra Angelico created a metaphysic of light out of Thomist doctrine, hence remotely Aristotelian in origin. These were the antithetic terms Piero synthesized in his painting.

*

At this stage in his evolution Fra Angelico succeeded in reconciling religion and science in art. As he had always put piety on a high intellectual level, his *docta pietas* could now rank with the loftiest thinking of the "philosophers," while adapting itself at the same time to the spiritual needs and compass of a society superbly conscious of its cultural superiority. The Dominican Order was then at the height of its prestige; Cosimo de' Medici had actively promoted its cause and now its destinies were guided by St Antoninus, one of the great churchmen of the time, who left many didactic writings intended to bolster the morals of the Florentine middle classes. To these same classes Alberti addressed his celebrated essay *On the Care of the Family*. The historical investigations of the humanists and the rules of conduct preconized by the powerful religious orders—both sought to lay the foundations of a better society and mold a world in gestation. Fra Angelico lived in the thick of these problems. His efforts to strike a balance between science and piety prove as much. Scrupling as he did to dishearten the flock by too intransigent a plea for chastened living and an austere faith, he prompted men to recognize God in their own experience of the world, or rather in a deeper experience of earthly life refined by meditation.

Dating from about the same time as the San Vincenzo di Annalena altarpiece is the *Coronation of the Virgin* (Louvre), executed for the church of San Domenico at Fiesole, a work with passages of great beauty and merit, but on the whole the most involved, ungainly and coldly rhetorical composition he ever painted. Yet the sharp contrasts between these two paintings seem quite natural when we allow for the variety of theme and key that runs through humanist literature, and for the fact that Fra Angelico was a scholarly painter whose art, more than most, readily adjusted itself to changing literary styles.

In his recent monograph on the artist (Phaidon Press, London, 1952), John Pope-Hennessy draws attention to the two different approaches to space representation in *The Coronation of the Virgin*: one perspective for the throne, tabernacle and steps, another for the tiled pavement in the foreground. On this account he infers that the altarpiece was only begun by Fra Angelico, the foreground and other passages as well being painted in afterwards by a younger artist, whom he tentatively identifies as Domenico Veneziano (Pope-Hennessy, *The Early Style of Domenico Veneziano, Burlington Magazine*, xciii, 1951, pp. 216-223). I cannot share this view. To my mind, the entire work is by Fra Angelico and what we really have here is a deliberate trick of perspective. The divergent viewpoints from which we see the scene are calculated to heighten the illusion of distance between the choir of angels and saints, on the one

THE CORONATION OF THE VIRGIN, DETAIL. ►
CA. 1430-1440. LOUVRE, PARIS.

hand, and Christ and the Virgin on the other, who thus stand dominant at the apex of the composition. The device is quite in keeping with the festive character of the work, replete with stage effects, and its distinctly worldly—not to say political—rather than sacred tenor. Hence what seems to me the idea underlying the painting: the necessity and indeed the intrinsic beauty of hierarchical order, not only on earth but also in heaven. It is not for nothing that these figures are the worldliest he ever painted; and the symbology ungainly, the tone blatantly oratorical, the whole inordinately solemn and ornate.

The other great composition couched in worldly, well-nigh political terms is *The Virgin enthroned with Eight Angels between Sts Lawrence, John the Evangelist, Mark, Cosmas, Damian, Dominic, Francis and Peter Martyr*. Here, too, the crush of figures and sumptuous trappings is such as can only be deliberate in intent. The setting is a garden, curtained off from the pleasant wood beyond by rich brocaded fabrics strung across the rear immediately behind the row of figures. The throne is the usual tabernacle, with a gorgeous oriental carpet spread before it, but the effect is rather that of a mediaeval love-court. As if he felt he had nothing more to lose, he pushed theatrical effect to the limit by stringing garlands across the top and tying up to either side what has all the earmarks of a stage curtain.

On the predella are *Scenes from the Life of Sts Cosmas and Damian*. These, too, illustrate the momentary, but highly significant conjunction of civil and sacred ideals in Fra Angelico's work. Here again, step by step, he follows the tale as it is told in *The Golden Legend*, but forgoing now the ingenuous tone we noted in the *Scenes from the Life of St Nicholas of Bari*, he rises all at once from fable to history, or, if you will, to hagiography,

◀   THE CORONATION OF THE VIRGIN, DETAIL.
CA. 1430-1440. LOUVRE, PARIS.

since we are obviously at a far cry from Alberti's notion of history. But for the first time, the artist seems to feel himself in the realm of actual historical fact. He made a point, first of all, of designing plausible architecture and landscape, then set his figures skillfully in movement at active moments, yet conferring on them a certain autonomy with respect to the scene and action. Here we see why light, without losing any of its

FRA ANGELICO AND HIS PUPILS: ST DOMINIC AND HIS COMPANIONS FED BY ANGELS. PREDELLA SCENE FROM THE CORONATION OF THE VIRGIN. CA. 1430-1440. LOUVRE, PARIS.

STS COSMAS AND DAMIAN MIRACULOUSLY REPLACING THE LEG
OF THE DEACON JUSTINIAN. PREDELLA SCENE FROM THE VIRGIN AND CHILD
ENTHRONED WITH SAINTS AND ANGELS. CA. 1437-1438. ($14\frac{1}{2} \times 17\frac{5}{8}$")
MUSEO DI SAN MARCO, FLORENCE.

supernatural "creaminess," adheres more intimately to objects, caresses and plumbs them, instead of lightly ricocheting over a succession of planes.

A glance at the wonderful view of a town in *The Burial of Sts Cosmas and Damian* will convince us of this, or at the

STS COSMAS AND DAMIAN THROWN INTO THE SEA AND SAVED BY AN ANGEL.
PREDELLA SCENE FROM THE VIRGIN AND CHILD
ENTHRONED WITH SAINTS AND ANGELS. CA. 1437-1438. $(7\frac{3}{4} \times 8\frac{5}{8}'')$
MUSEO DI SAN MARCO, FLORENCE.

architectural background with oblique lighting in *Sts Cosmas and Damian appearing before Lysias*. Figures are no longer rooted in the narrative, and their autonomy coincides with greater freedom in the unfolding of the episodes, with a new alacrity

THE BURIAL OF STS COSMAS AND DAMIAN AND THEIR BROTHERS.
PREDELLA SCENE FROM THE VIRGIN AND CHILD ENTHRONED WITH SAINTS
AND ANGELS. CA. 1437-1438. ($14\frac{1}{2} \times 17\frac{5}{8}''$)
MUSEO DI SAN MARCO, FLORENCE.

of movement and an intensified localization of light effects.
Instead of inviting our guileless admiration of a well-performed
miracle, he brings to bear a keenly observant eye and objectively
presents us with natural events.

The Descent from the Cross dates from roundabout 1440. Now housed in the Museo di San Marco at Florence, it stood originally in the church of Santa Trinità at Florence. Painted on a large wooden panel whose three finials had already been decorated by Lorenzo Monaco, this was Fra Angelico's first large-scale "historical" picture, with an actual happening as its theme. In it he seems bent on showing how far a scene from sacred history—for him, that is, an event purely allegorical in value—differs from events of secular history. Yet he insists on perfect unity between religious content and natural forms, with the unexpected result (perhaps involuntary) that he forthwith creates a kind of classico-Christian myth whose poetic elevation has no counterpart in humanist religious literature.

His point of departure is perhaps still the cultural, and in a sense social, motives that in these years directed his efforts. He aimed at showing that common ground lay between the Christian ideal of the Church and the intellectual ideal of the humanists; that poetry was far from being the exclusive preserve of the classical writers; that religious faith may also be expressed in forms that are not necessarily naïve and popular in their appeal.

Even a brief analysis of the figure-groups and lay-out of *The Descent from the Cross* will show us something of the careful planning and deliberation that went into this picture, as into all his art. On the right, placidly exchanging a few words, dressed in the quaint, half-ancient, half-mediaeval fashion of which Fra Angelico was so fond, are four or five bystanders, one of them holding up the crown of thorns and the nails, symbols of the Passion. They have the look of actual portraits; one is known to represent Michelozzo, the architect and sculptor who restored the convent of San Marco. Except for the youth in front who has knelt down in worshipful prayer, these are "philosophers" who see not the *reality* of the event taking place beneath their eyes, but its *symbolical* side. They stand for *docta pietas*, the religion of the mind, the faith of the humanists. As against this, on the left, we have a devout group of women in fervent prayer come to receive and gently, lovingly shroud the dead Christ. They betoken *caritas*, the piety of the poor in spirit, the religion of the heart.

THE DESCENT FROM THE CROSS. CA. 1440. (69¼ × 72¾")
MUSEO DI SAN MARCO, FLORENCE.

THE DESCENT FROM THE CROSS. DETAIL FROM THE RIGHT SIDE.
MUSEO DI SAN MARCO, FLORENCE.

Both, however, revere Christ "the true God, the true man,"
whose limply arching body, lowered from the Cross, bridges the
two groups. Though it bears the stigmata of martyrdom, his body
betrays no sign of desecration, nor is it yet livid and stiffened in

THE DESCENT FROM THE CROSS. DETAIL FROM THE RIGHT SIDE. ▶
MUSEO DI SAN MARCO, FLORENCE.

death. The silver light of a spring morning bathes an almost Apollonian trunk and limbs and puts the ghost of a smile on these barely parted lips, veiling the features in an expression of unspeakable gentleness. This *Descent from the Cross*, symbolizing men's reverent piety towards a God who redeemed them with His life's blood, is like a Second Coming, a rebirth, a

THE DESCENT FROM THE CROSS. DETAIL FROM THE LEFT SIDE.
MUSEO DI SAN MARCO, FLORENCE.

"Renaissance." No work better supports Burdach's thesis to the effect that the Renaissance implicitly defines the true Christian meaning of palingenesis, a reawakening of the soul. Our Lord is lowered from the Cross in springtime, in the pure, limpid light of reawakening nature. The bitter tragedy of Calvary is only alluded to symbolically in a ledge of bare rock breaking the soft carpet of flowers and grass. In the background, to either side, as far as the eye can see, is one of the finest landscapes Fra Angelico ever painted, perhaps the first true landscape in 15th-century Italian painting.

Within the limits of this "religious naturalism," now so clearly delineated, no divergence can arise between natural light and the supernatural light that emanates from God. Flowing from object to object, light is continuously propagated from color to color. It flows steadily in even waves, form modeled all the while by evenly applied highlights. The focal point here, where light converges and whence it radiates, is the body of Christ in the center; and this intense concentration of light arises simply from the fact that His figure, instead of looming up against the open landscape, is framed by the color masses of the men holding it and stands out all the more sharply against the immediate, abstract geometry of the yellow ladders and the yellow Cross that bars the blue sky beyond. Here is natural light fulfilling its peculiar spatial function. The body of Christ marks the rhythmic peak of the composition, co-ordinates the surge of masses and leads the "choir" of secondary figures. For this type of historical composition is typically "choral" in character, progressing not by isolated figures dotted here and there, but by figure-groups compactly massed. What other distinction could Fra Angelico draw between secular history and religious history, if not this, that the first is the history of great persons taken singly, and of individual deeds, the second that of all mankind?

The Lamentation over the Dead Christ (Museo di San Marco, Florence) may be regarded as the ideal sequence to *The Descent from the Cross*, though the strong mythical flavor of the latter has been sublimated into unmingled poignancy, the very colors conveying a grief without name. Unwittingly perhaps, this treatment of history as an expression of collective pathos harks

THE LAMENTATION OVER THE DEAD CHRIST, DETAIL.
MUSEO DI SAN MARCO, FLORENCE.

THE LAMENTATION OVER THE DEAD CHRIST. 1440-1445. $(42\frac{1}{2} \times 64\frac{3}{4}'')$
MUSEO DI SAN MARCO, FLORENCE.

back to its initiator in painting: Giotto. In the compassionate
choir of kneeling figures encircling Christ's prostrate form,
we read into each face a particular accent of grief. The mediation
of nature between man and God is a thing of the past; above
and beyond the soothing emotions induced by nature open
depths of pure moral feelings. Considerably scaled down, the
landscape grows stark and remote; the Cross rises up like an
everlasting symbol of pain, whilst the impregnable walls of a
town stretch into the distance, as if to remind us that earthly
life is a barrier to piety and true faith.

In *The Entombment* (Alte Pinakothek, Munich) the dead Christ is brought almost brazenly forward as a pure symbol; the humbly reverent gestures of the Virgin and St John become purely ritual, while the landscape is whittled to a bare rock, all color subdued, all light dry and sparse. The more tightly the figures are bound in their contours, as if shrinking from contact with nature, the more contours grow expressive, overwrought, yet tender. This painting no longer drives home any thesis. Heedless of all else, it follows its own meditative way. Here we reach a climax in Fra Angelico's art; we feel him beset by a crisis of asceticism and self-mortification.

WORKS

II

FRESCOS AND LAST WORKS

FRESCOS AND LAST WORKS

IN 1436 Cosimo de' Medici requisitioned the dilapidated Silvrestrine convent of San Marco at Florence and handed it over to the Observant Dominicans. The architect and sculptor Michelozzo was entrusted with the work of rebuilding, which went ahead fairly rapidly, the church being ceremoniously dedicated by Pope Eugenius IV in 1443. The paintings, overseen and in part executed by Fra Angelico, may thus plausibly be held to date from about 1440 to 1447, in which year the art was summoned to Rome.

This extensive series of frescos, many of them painte in the cells on themes congenial to self-communion, with no regard for decoration, is a landmark in the history of religious thought. It is the formal acknowledgment that, above and beyond its long-accepted didactic function, painting might serve as a guide to meditation, as an instrument of knowledge and religious insight. Thus it was the concept of art's intellectual value that gave rise to this painting, which may justifiably be regarded as the crowning expression of 15th-century man's religious aspirations.

On the whole, these frescos tend towards a specific, well-defined end. It is only reasonable to suppose that St Antoninus, then Prior of the convent, had a voice in dictating the tenor of the work. But more than his hierarchical superior, he was also a close friend of the painter. As for the story of Fra Angelico's having been asked by the pope to accept the archbishopric of Florence but declining in favor of St Antoninus, even if we make allowance for Vasari's notorious way of peddling mere legends, it seems at least to vouch for the authority wielded

◀ CHRIST ON THE CROSS ADORED BY ST DOMINIC. FRESCO, AFTER 1437. (133½ × 60¾") CLOISTER, CONVENT OF SAN MARCO, FLORENCE.

by the artist both within and without the monastery. We may thus assume that, to a very large extent, the San Marco frescos reflect his own, his innermost religious convictions.

His appeal had hitherto gone to laymen, who saw little beyond the things of this world. His theme had been that salvation is attainable through earthly experience wisely guided, since after all God created this world and a "good" soul, if alive to the beauty of Creation, is also alive to the beauty of the Creator. But at San Marco he was painting for monks, for men who had renounced the world for closer communion with God through prayer, meditation and ascetic practices. In such an art nature need no longer mediate between the soul and God, nor need contemplation any longer depend for its efficacy on a chain of logic working back from effect to cause. And as nature lost her function and her interest, so too did history lose hers. Personal events cease to mark the monkish life; all that matters is observance of the Rule, which if followed to the letter is a warranty of salvation. Thus it is that scarcely a painting by Fra Angelico has come down to us in which some Dominican saint is not vigilantly present, a constant admonition to abide by the Rule of the Order.

No longer sermonizing now, but admonishing his brethren *ex cathedra*, he turned off the old flow of eloquence, spontaneous in appearance but in reality worked out with painstaking care. Henceforward he confined himself to suggesting themes of meditation and enunciating the mysteries of the faith, and his naturalistic allegories turned into pure symbols. In so doing, Fra Angelico demonstrated his power of laying symbols bare and creating forms that immaterially conveyed the symbol's ideational force.

ST DOMINIC. DETAIL FROM CHRIST ON THE CROSS ADORED BY ST DOMINIC. ▶
FRESCO, AFTER 1437. CLOISTER, CONVENT OF SAN MARCO, FLORENCE.

Almost at once, with *Christ on the Cross adored by St Dominic* in the convent cloister, we get the pattern of this Dominican devoutness, which betrays neither blinding ecstasy nor ascetic mortification. On the contrary, it is the mind's concentration on the truth of the faith, a *contractio animi* diametrically opposed to the clashing forces of history. The features of St Dominic are the very prototype of a physiognomy into which the devout soul has rushed: the knitted brows, the tense set of the jaws, the intent gaze, the quivering of the lips, the dilated nostrils, the faint shaking of the hands as they brush against the blood-streaked wood of the Cross. This man is "the mirror of true penitence." Again, we have only to compare the aforementioned *Descent from the Cross* with *The Crucifixion* in the chapter house to realize the thoroughness with which, at San Marco, history, nature and myth have been ruled out in favor of rite and symbol. First of all, dismiss the thought that the red ground of *The Crucifixion* is a lurid sunset beyond Calvary; it is simply the rough coat of plaster left bare by the crumbling away of the original blue overpainting. Mentally restoring the blue ground against which the figures originally stood out, we see that this is no longer an event of the remote past reconstituted in the painter's imagination, but the image of a sacrifice repeated anew each day in Christian rite, while the saints in prayer are ministers to the act, not mute witnesses to a scene of suffering. Except for an overwrought accent here and there, and the stock device of alternating figures standing and kneeling, which imbues the composition with a vague impression of sweep and movement, this steadfast body of saints keeping vigil at the foot of the three crosses is a unique expression of unshakable faith, whose militancy we faintly sense.

◄　　THE CRUCIFIXION, DETAIL. FRESCO, AFTER 1437.
CHAPTER HOUSE, CONVENT OF SAN MARCO, FLORENCE.

In the corridors on the first floor of the convent Fra Angelico painted two frescos: *The Annunciation* and *The Virgin and Child enthroned with Sts Dominic, Cosmas, Damian, Mark, John the Evangelist, Thomas Aquinas, Lawrence and Peter Martyr.* In both, the classical rigor of the architecture may be accounted for by his close association with Michelozzo, the most humanist-minded of all 15th-century Florentine architects.

The loggia shown in *The Annunciation* is designed in strict accordance with the rules of perspective, though the figures seem reluctant to fit into it. Beyond the two large arches facing us, the composition is built up along slanting planes in recession. The vanishing point of the Virgin's figure lands at the far end of the loggia; the angel's runs through the open door to the wall beyond. Thus their vanishing lines intersect. The laws of symmetry are only slightly infringed, yet sufficiently for the loggia to be no longer a "place" or "setting," but a pure geometrical form, an enclosure of white, abstract light contrasting with the semi-darkness of the landscape. The source of light is not in nature, but in the figures, and these, instead of being framed in space, stand out in full light, to which they lend their own life, their own body; thus devoid of physical volume, they somehow acquire the strange concreteness of "true" things. The rough-hewn stool on which the Virgin is seated contrasts sharply with the classical elegance of the columns and capitals; it is the symbol of the slight but deliberate gap between the space dimension and that of the figures. Because of this gap, the loggia appears as a pure geometric form, devoid as it is of actual weight and substance; or as a pure "historical" form, a vague classical souvenir of the episode. So too the figures, for all their immateriality, become pure human forms. And out

THE CRUCIFIXION, DETAIL. FRESCO, AFTER 1437.
CHAPTER HOUSE, CONVENT OF SAN MARCO, FLORENCE. ▶

THE VIRGIN AND CHILD ENTHRONED WITH STS DOMINIC, COSMAS, DAMIAN, MARK, JOHN THE EVANGELIST, THOMAS AQUINAS, LAWRENCE AND PETER MARTYR, DETAIL. FRESCO, AFTER 1437. CONVENT OF SAN MARCO, FLORENCE.

of a composition whose colors and linework are so tightly knit, so minutely calculated, emerges the idealized face of the Virgin, refined, transparent, intent, the exemplary reflection of beauty no longer earthbound, but wholly spiritual and free.

The altarpiece executed for the church of the Franciscan convent of San Buonaventura at Bosco ai Frati (now in the Museo di San Marco at Florence) marks the transition from the large altarpieces painted to the glory of the Virgin and the fresco on the same theme in the upper corridor of San Marco. In the San Buonaventura altarpiece the architectural background, severely humanist in character, consists of niches and columns into which the throne fits and becomes in turn a niche whose luminous cavity links the half-circle of saints and angels with the backdrop. In the San Marco fresco the scene shifts, taking place before a smooth white wall, broken only in the center by the slight recess of the throne and marked off at regular intervals by Corinthian half-columns. The long thin shadows flung by the latter show that the wall is swept by oblique lighting; it is no more than a backdrop whose abstract, geometrical proportions and bright tonality give it a much higher, much more immaterial light intensity than is to be got with gold grounds. The two files of saints are strung out to either side like wings; they coincide with the vanishing lines that end up in the center in the person of the Virgin. All these figures are lit up indirectly by the wall. What we have here are two opposing spatial layouts, whose sole meeting point is the Virgin herself, who belongs to the luminous plane of the background and forms the apex of the two files of saints. Looking out between the blue of the mantle and the sparkling gold of the nimbus, her face is the focus of maximum light intensity and the climax of both spatial edifices. Here again, owing to the slight gap between two perspectives, the abstract, geometrical notion of space, together with the light that so perfectly merges with pure white, produces a greater clarity, distinctness and autonomy in the figures. Each seems to take refuge in its own contour-lines, independent of the others except for the uniform fashion in which they stand out against the background.

Fortunately, no heaviness mars these forms. On the contrary, as the contours isolate the color-masses and tighten them up, the colors themselves grow softer, more subdued and aerial, sheering away all weight. Modeling grows softer and dimmer within forms; the narrative description becomes summary in the extreme, proceeding by allusions. The depth of a gaze or the firm cut of a face—these are enough to reveal spiritual beauty, just as they do in the Virgin of *The Annunciation*.

The frescos in the cells display an even greater economy or asceticism. The colloquy between painter and spectator takes place on a more intimate level—that of the confessional, we might almost say. The last echoes of worldly life, the last vestiges of nature herself, have vanished in *The Adoration of the Magi*, painted in the cell reserved for Cosimo de' Medici. Here we may discern a discreet allusion, if not to the magnanimity shown by Cosimo to the Dominicans of San Marco, at least to the homage the great of the earth may fitly pay to the God born of a virgin mother in a village manger. But as if to remind faltering spirits that once within the convent walls, they have left the world behind them for good, he painted a bitter landscape of burnt-out mountains before the picturesque procession of figures, a landscape livid under a white, gritty light. This is the earth which, to lay eyes, is a garden-place in springtime; it is but dust and stone to those who embrace the Dominican rule of life: "Every pleasure has its source in God. There is no pleasure that comes not from Him."

THE ANNUNCIATION, DETAIL. FRESCO, AFTER 1437.
CELL, CONVENT OF SAN MARCO, FLORENCE.

▶

93

THE ANNUNCIATION. FRESCO, AFTER 1437.
$(73\frac{1}{2} \times 65\frac{1}{2}'')$
CELL, CONVENT OF SAN MARCO, FLORENCE.

CHRIST SCORNED. FRESCO, AFTER 1437.
$(76\frac{1}{2} \times 62\frac{1}{2}'')$
CELL, CONVENT OF SAN MARCO, FLORENCE.

95

Ang. 41

THE TRANSFIGURATION. FRESCO, AFTER 1437.
$(74\frac{1}{4} \times 62\frac{1}{2}'')$
CELL, CONVENT OF SAN MARCO, FLORENCE.

We get some insight into the why and wherefore of this unrelieved asceticism if we compare *The Annunciation* in the upper corridor, referred to a moment ago, with that in one of the cells—that in Cell 3, to be exact. In the latter even the parallel between abstract space and natural space has been done away with. The scene takes place in a loggia of the convent

THE TRANSFIGURATION, DETAIL. FRESCO, AFTER 1437.
CELL, CONVENT OF SAN MARCO, FLORENCE.

represented in an axial perspective that kills both shadows and foreshortenings. Even so, the vaulting at the top of the picture, light strips alternating with dark, is an allusion to the passage of white light that is all but swallowed up in the stark geometry of space, and yet is perceptibly tinted with the colors of the bodies through which it flashes as if they were quite transparent. A picture space that neither contains nor locates, a light that neither lights up nor models—if such is Fra Angelico's ideal, it is certainly not attainable by the customary avenues of human knowledge, or by any deductive reasoning from effect to cause. Only contemplation and the ascetic life lead finally and surely to truth, which is cause, without pausing in the byways of the real world, which is effect.

We need entertain no illusions as to the mystical garden in the *Noli me tangere.* Far from denoting a revival of interest in nature, it exists for purely iconographical reasons and is quite untouched by any of the light emanating from Christ, a white and colorless flow of light that bathes Mary Magdalen as she kneels before Him. From now on this painting assumes all the stark conviction of a verse from the Bible, and symbolic meaning underlies each image. But like a symbol, each image conveys a truth of its own, a certitude, a deep life of its own, whose sense no analogy or comparison with natural things will yield. Into faces and gestures we read a message of human pain and suffering that gives us an inkling of a man's intensely concentrated struggle against the temptations of this world before he finally contemplated the unutterable symbols matter masks. The merest hints tell the story: a penetrating glance, an outstretched hand, an all but imperceptible tremor of this white, supernal light as its brushes against bodies. Here is where Fra Angelico reverts to Giotto—not to his stately construction in terms of masses, but to those keen, impromptu-seeming accents of poignant emotion that are the deepest, most human side of his art. What henceforth lends Fra Angelico's figures a semblance of concrete reality, even though they no longer inhabit this world, is the fact that he forgoes now anything smacking of the miraculous. Being a perceptible—and in a sense naturalistic—manifestation of the divine presence, miracles are the layman's metaphor for God, whereas now a dogmatic statement of doctrine was called for.

As regards supreme truth, *docta ignorantia* stands on a more or less equal footing with *docta pietas*, much as the meek and the mighty stand on a par and class distinctions, respectfully observed in political and social spheres, die out within the religious community. Perhaps these points should guide us in our approach to Fra Angelico's "meditation" on *Christ scorned*, in which a whole set of folk symbols is grafted on to a schematic lay-out so pure and rarefied that it is no longer space, but simply a geometrical figure. Something more than space, indeed, is this straightforward system of lines and planes defining an abstract dimension in which Christ is monumentally framed—a figure that seems to revive the purest, solidest forms of Giotto. Nothing is simpler than the rigorous geometry of this composition, built up round an equilateral triangle whose apex is the head of Christ, the base angles being the figures of the Virgin and St Dominic. From these two strongly modeled figures the eye lifts naturally to the pillar of light formed by Christ. And if this highly accurate geometric handling of space in terms of light bespeaks an effort to fathom Giotto's structural secrets and put them to use in conjunction with the new techniques of perspective, *The Presentation in the Temple* shows him pressing his analysis well beyond the merely formal aspects of his great elder's art; it shows him striking to the very roots, to the moral essence of Giotto's painting.

The intense pursuit of moral truths, and the doctrinarian faith that incited him to pursue them—this it was that led

Ang. 43

Fra Angelico to transcend the allegorical naturalism that he
had himself formulated. Several works bring this out. Compare,
for example, *The Coronation of the Virgin* in the Louvre with the
fresco on the same theme in the convent of San Marco. In the

latter Christ and the Virgin are no more than luminous forms hovering in the great white light of the upper background, while beneath them kneeling saints in prayer humbly signify an intrusion of earthly things into this celestial region. Between the later and the earlier *Coronation* lies the gulf between a glimpse of paradise and a fanciful yearning for it, necessarily expressed in naturalistic terms (as it is again in *The Last Judgment*). Or compare *The Descent from the Cross* discussed above with *The Transfiguration* at San Marco in which the hieratic figure of Christ stands out in white against white before an immense egg- or almond-shaped blob of light, His arms outstretched in the threefold gesture of martyrdom, compassion and creation (one of the very few "mandalas" that western art has succeeded in creating). The prophets and saints encircling him seem to merge with the rocky mount, as if to show that a single distinction counts: that which separates matter from light and creatures from the Creator. Here we realize how vastly pure symbol differs from naturalistic allegory, and the contemplation of dogma from the invention of classico-Christian myths, however poetic and appealing they may be.

*

In the Chapel of Nicholas V at the Vatican, working from 1447 on in collaboration with Benozzo Gozzoli and other pupils of his, Fra Angelico painted six large frescos relating *Scenes from the Life of St Stephen and St Lawrence*. The pontificate of Nicholas V (1447-1455), himself an eminent scholar and a great friend of letters, saw the Catholic Church at last swept into the orbit of humanist culture. "All the scholars in the world," wrote Vespasiano, "flocked to Rome in the time of Pope Nicholas."

◀ THE CORONATION OF THE VIRGIN. FRESCO, AFTER 1437. (74¼ × 62½″)
CELL, CONVENT OF SAN MARCO, FLORENCE.

And, indeed, the restoration of classical learning, literature and art now went hand in hand with the business of the Church. Into this worldly, but highly refined atmosphere Fra Angelico was summoned by the pope himself and commissioned to revive the traditions of the early martyrs and confessors, the "ancients" of the Primitive Church, and near-contemporaries, moreover, of the philosophers and poets whose works were stirring the humanists to lay the moral bases of a new life.

But surely it was not the high station of his new sponsors alone that led Fra Angelico to create what we might call his "Latin works." We may take it for granted that he could never have achieved such gravity of tone, so acute an awareness of historical values, without the intense religious experience afforded by his work at San Marco. There he forswore every link with the world and sought out an immediate relation between man and God unaffected by the physical intermediary of natural things—an immediate relation, that is, between human ethics, which translate man's aspirations to the good, and God, the supreme good. He had thus discovered that there is something far deeper in man than natural appearances and feelings. Thereafter he ceased to draw on this natural well of forms and content so as the better to show humanity and godhead as two quite distinct worlds, but worlds tending always to become one by virtue of man's aspiration to the good and God's infinite compassion for his sins and tribulations. In the cells at San Marco, insofar as it lay within his power to do so, he gave expression to the divine; in the Chapel of Nicholas V, to the human, to the deep-seated moral impulse towards the good, which also determines actions and can therefore fitly provide the stuff of history.

◀ ST LAWRENCE BEFORE DECIUS, DETAIL. FRESCO, CA. 1447-1455. CHAPEL OF NICHOLAS V, VATICAN.

ST LAWRENCE RECEIVING THE TREASURES
OF THE CHURCH FROM POPE SIXTUS II. FRESCO, CA. 1447-1455.
CHAPEL OF NICHOLAS V, VATICAN.

ST LAWRENCE DISTRIBUTING ALMS.
FRESCO, CA. 1447-1455.
CHAPEL OF NICHOLAS V, VATICAN.

"Love thy neighbor as thyself"—this is the precept of the religious life, and this is the theme of the Vatican frescos. It was not chosen at random. Under Nicholas V the Schism was finally healed when the Antipope Felix V resigned his pretensions in 1449. The Church consolidated her oecumenical authority against the separatist spirit of the national churches and to a large degree reinstituted the universality of the Primitive Latin Church. From now on there could no longer be any clash between sacred ideals and humanist ideals. The distribution of "alms" shown twice over in the Vatican frescos is much more than an appeal for charity. We have only to study the noble classicism of these "beggars" to see that they symbolize something much deeper: the "mystical body" of the Church in the shape of the entire community of the faithful. To this "mystical body," after long dark centuries, the Church owed its "renaissance."

These frescos are a far cry from the naïvely edifying predella scenes and their mythology of the miraculous. The theme is action itself, but symbolic action whose scope far exceeds the event on which it hinges, and whose repercussions proved far-reaching, they being precisely those taking effect in the glorious days of Nicholas' pontificate. It was only natural that Fra Angelico, overstepping the bounds of his religious naturalism and his ascetic symbolism, should now revert to the master of his youth. On the threshold of old age, he gratefully turned back to Masaccio in search of the fundamentals of a new ethical conception of life, back to the painter who had guided his early approach to a "naturalistic" vision of things. Now at last he recognized Masaccio for what he was: the harbinger of new aspirations, of an ideal of self-expression that in no way clashed with the Christian ideal of life.

If, in the Vatican frescos, the architectural grounds as well as many secondary figures may reasonably be ascribed to

Benozzo Gozzoli, the design and spirit of the work are Fra Angelico's alone. The lay-out of the scenes is proof of this. Witness the impeccable application of perspective around a vertical wall in the center, whose dual function is to divide each fresco in half and to bind the two halves in unison, exactly as in the early predella scenes. But never before had architecture

THE MARTYRDOM OF ST LAWRENCE, DETAIL. FRESCO, CA. 1447-1455.
CHAPEL OF NICHOLAS V, VATICAN.

bulked so large in his art; no longer a mere setting or a background, its masses and volumes compete with the figures for the leading role. The ease and power with which Fra Angelico organizes these volumes in space, so vigorously articulates these planes, and distributes full and empty spaces across the picture surface are matched nowhere but in the frescos of the Brancacci Chapel. Take the desolate stretch of shore and landscape in *The Stoning of St Stephen*, with the receding line of bleak trees; its only ancestor is the landscape in Masaccio's *Tribute Money*. From Masaccio, too, derive the grouping and distribution of figures in such a way as to impress upon us that, while remaining "choral" and turning on masses, the action reaches its dramatic climax in the gesture of the protagonists. From him again comes the weighting down of masses we find in the squatting women of *St Stephen preaching*, or the legless beggar in *St Lawrence distributing Alms*, or certain compact, thickset, foreshortened figures, such as that of the officiating priest in *The Ordination of St Stephen*.

He no longer drew his subject-matter from the ingenuous tales of *The Golden Legend*, but from the austere commentaries of the *Acta Sanctorum*, and from now on he looked to history for moral edification and as an inducement to the good life, as one hope of salvation.

This new awareness, then, of values that give meaning to life and human action led Fra Angelico back to Masaccio. We might add that, in some measure at least, it also reconciled him with Alberti. Not with the Alberti of the treatise on painting, but rather with the man who, in the mature phase of a mellow humanism, while serving at the Papal Court at the very same time as Fra Angelico, had embarked on the writing of his ten-volume treatise *De Architectura*. The deeply receding naves of *The Ordination of St Lawrence* and *St Lawrence distributing Alms*, the flawlessly classical architecture in the background of

St Lawrence before Decius and *The Martyrdom of St Lawrence*—
these are no longer the fanciful settings of the predella scenes,
convenient devices for locating the action in strange lands of
the remote past; they are a deliberate, minutely accurate recon-
stitution of classical Antiquity, worthy of the best produced
by humanism, which was now a force to be reckoned with,
one destined to play a vitalizing role in modern life and art.

*

Historically speaking, the great cycle of Fra Angelico's
painting comes to an end with the Vatican frescos and their
avowal of humanist principles. As for the angels and prophets
in glory, painted in 1447 in collaboration with Benozzo Gozzoli
on the ceiling of the Cappella di San Brizio in Orvieto Cathedral,
they distinctly cut the figure of literary pieces, conventional
examples of church decoration.

Fra Angelico returned to Florence in 1449 to accept the post
of Prior of San Marco, which he held for the usual term of three
years. The duties incumbent on him, we may assume, left him
relatively little time for painting, since only a few "minor"
works have come down to us from this period, chief of which is
a set of thirty-five *Scenes from the Life of Christ* that went to
decorate the doors of a silver chest in the Florentine church of
the Santissima Annunziata; they are now in the Museo di San
Marco. Several of his pupils—notably Alesso Baldovinetti—
took a hand in the work, which inaugurates a new type of
religious painting unashamedly popular in its appeal. In one
sense these small panels prefigure the tracts and canticles of
another great Dominican, Savonarola (though quite free of the
latter's polemical aggressiveness, needless to add). On a doctrinarian woof, with great formal skill and inventiveness, Fra
Angelico interwove orthodox subject-matter, structural rhythms
and popular motifs, deliberately setting his themes in a key

THE ANNUNCIATION. PANEL FROM SCENES OF THE LIFE OF CHRIST. AFTER 1450. (CA. 15¼ × 15¼″) MUSEO DI SAN MARCO, FLORENCE.

faintly archaic and maintaining the monodic line of the narrative, above which rises now and then a sharper note, a flash of typically Florentine wit.

In the charming nightscape of *The Nativity*, the body of the Christchild shines forth like a lamp, lighting up the lean-to beneath which he lies. In *The Flight into Egypt*, the Virgin sits athwart the wily-looking mule as if she were enthroned. In *The Presentation in the Temple* and *Christ teaching in the Temple*, the architecture gives rise to involved and rather harsh plays of light. Even the colors have been reduced to their simplest tones, though with no attendant sacrifice of their luminous intensity. Thus Fra Angelico readily adjusts the cadence of the narrative to the easy, lightly falling rhythm congenial to the popular mind.

If by and large he reverted to Trecento compositional schemes, he did so for the same reasons that were to prompt Savonarola to re-echo the lyrics of Jacopone da Todi. Both of them harked back to the *"biblia pauperum,"* to the complaisant, didactic, occasionally sententious spirit of the catechism, from which, moreover, these paintings retain both the easy formalism and the doctrinarian rigor. And just as in Savonarola's lyrical eloquence, the utter simplicity of the narrative and its lilting cadence in no wise detract from the depth of feeling behind them, on the contrary. *The Massacre of the Innocents*, in fact, is one of the most tragic, one of the most heart-rending scenes in all 15th-century Italian painting. Dating from these same years, the *Crucifixion* in the Fogg Art Museum shows the heights to which Fra Angelico was capable of rising in the way of pure poetry.

Folk humor and didactic solemnity go hand in hand in the *Last Judgment* (Galleria Nazionale, Rome), painted presumably in the convent of Santa Maria sopra Minerva in Rome, and regarded by some as the master's last work. This would seem to be a restatement of an earlier composition on the same theme, of which two replicas, safely ascribable to pupils, are now in the Museo di San Marco, Florence, and the Kaiser Friedrich Museum, Berlin.

PAGE 112: THE LAST JUDGMENT, THE ASCENSION AND PENTECOST, CENTRAL PANEL. CA. 1450. (29 × 14¼″) GALLERIA NAZIONALE D'ARTE ANTICA, ROME.

But the historical cycle of Fra Angelico's art concluded, as we have said, with the Vatican frescos. In these we see the junction of the two main trends of 15th-century Italian painting, one religious, the other humanistic. That the avowed Thomism to which Fra Angelico looked for a renewal of taste—while Alberti hoped to bring this about on a neo-Platonic basis—was not a belated appeal to lifeless traditions is amply proved by subsequent developments in 15th-century Tuscan painting. Nothing, moreover, would be farther from the truth than to believe that in the early 15th century Aristotelian and Platonic traditions stood in open conflict. The revolution of ideas that we call the Renaissance arose not from the clash of these two traditions, but from a conscious striving to trace them back to their sources and reintegrate them dialectically into a clear conception of Antiquity. What we have sought to bring out here is the role that fell to Fra Angelico in the rise of the new culture, a role no less significant than that which we credit to the great creators of that culture.

SELECTED BIBLIOGRAPHY

INDEX OF NAMES
AND BIOGRAPHICAL NOTICES

CONTENTS

SELECTED BIBLIOGRAPHY

Source Works

Filippo BALDINUCCI, *Notizie*, I, 1768, p. 401 ff. — Giovanni GAYE, *Carteggio inedito d'artisti dei secoli XIV, XV, XVI*, Florence 1839-1840. — Vincenzo MARCHESE, *Memorie dei più insigni pittori, scultori ed architetti domenicani*, 2nd edition, Florence 1854; id., *San Marco, Convento dei Padri Predicatori in Firenze, illustrato e inciso principalmente nei dipinti del B. G. Angelico, con la vita dello stesso pittore*, Florence 1853. — Giorgio VASARI, *Vite*, 1878, II, p. 505 ff. — Antonio MANETTI, *Uomini singolari in Firenze del MCCCC inanzi*, in *Operette istoriche...*, edited by Milanesi, Florence 1887. — *Codice Magliabechiano*, edited by Carl Frey, 1892. — Antonio BILLI, *Il Libro di Antonio Billi*, edited by Carl Frey, 1892.

Monographs

A.W. von SCHLEGEL, *Johann von Fiesole*, Leipzig 1846. — Ernst FOERSTER, *Leben und Werke des Fra Giovanni Angelico da Fiesole*, 1861. — E. DOBBERT, *Fra Angelico da Fiesole*, 1878, I, pp. 80-94. — SWESSTER, *Fra Angelico*, Boston 1879. — C. PHILLIMORE, *Fra Angelico*, London 1881. — Domenico TUMIATI, *Fra Angelico*, Florence 1897. — I. B. SUPINO, *Beato Angelico*, Florence 1898; id., in THIEME-BECKER, *Künstler-Lexikon*, I, p. 516. — S. BEISSEL, *Fra Giovanni Angelico*, Freiburg-im-Breisgau 1895. — BROUSSOLE, *La critique mystique et Fra Angelico*, Paris 1898; id., *Fra Angelico*, Paris 1902. — V. CRAWFORD, *Fra Angelico*, London 1900. — Langton DOUGLAS, *Fra Angelico*, London 1901. — E. CARTIER, *Vie de Fra Angelico de Fiesole*, Paris 1902. — NIEUWBARN, *Fra Angelico*, Leyden 1901. — Walter ROTHES, *Die Darstellung des Fra Giovanni Angelico aus dem Leben Christi und Mariae*, Strasbourg 1902. — E. STALEY, *Fra Angelico*, London n.d. — Gaston SORTAIS, *Fra Angelico et Benozzo Gozzoli*, Lille-Paris 1905. — NEWNESS, *Fra Angelico*, London 1906. — H. C. COCHIN, *Le Bienheureux Fra Angelico da Fiesole*, Paris 1906. — Alois WURM, *Meister- und Schülerarbeit in Fra Angelicos Werk*, Strasbourg 1907. — Angelo SERAFINI, *L'epopea cristiana nei dipinti di Beato Angelico, con appendice di documenti...*, Orvieto 1911. — Antonio ZUCCATO, *Fra Angelico da Fiesole*, Vincenza 1913. — I. M. STRUNK, *Beato Angelico*, Munich 1913; id., *Fra Angelico aus dem Dominikaner Orden*, Munich 1916. — A. PICHON, *Fra Angelico*, Paris 1922. — Frieda SCHOTTMÜLLER, *Fra Angelico da Fiesole*, Stuttgart & Leipzig 1924. — Clara CIRAOLO & B. Maria ARBIB, *Beato Angelico*, Bergamo 1925. — Roberto PAPINI, *Fra Giovanni Angelico*, Bologna 1925. — Max WINGENROTH, *Angelico da Fiesole*, Leipzig 1926. — Paul MURATOFF, *Frate Angelico*, Rome 1930. — Edouard SCHNEIDER, *Fra*

Angelico da Fiesole, Paris 1933. — Pio CIUTI, *Il Beato Angelico*, Florence 1940. — Achille BERTINI-CALOSSO, *Il Beato Angelico e la pittura umbra*, Spoleto 1940. — Germain BAZIN, *Fra Angelico*, Paris 1949. — Piero BARGELLINI, *La pittura ascetica del Beato Angelico*, Rome 1952. — John POPE-HENNESSY, *Fra Angelico*, London 1952. — Anna BANTI, *Fra Angelico*, Milan 1953.

Critical Articles

Max WINGENROTH, *Beiträge zur Angelico Forschung*, in *Repertorium für Kunstwissenschaft*, XXI, 1898, p. 335 ff. — Abbé AURIOL, *De Fra Angelico*, in *Revue Thomiste*, 1898. — P. MANTZ, *Fra Angelico da Fiesole*, in *Gazette des Beaux-Arts*, I, 1859, pp. 193-206. — H. DELABORDE, *Fra Angelico da Fiesole*, in *Etudes*, I, 1864, pp. 92-133. — Adolfo VENTURI, *Beato Angelico e Benozzo Gozzoli*, in *L'Arte*, 1901, pp. 1-29; id., in *Storia dell'Arte italiana*, VII, I. — Umberto CLÉRISSAC, *Fra Angelico et le Surnaturel*, in *Revue Thomiste*, 1901. — Jules HELBIG, *La Critique mystique et Fra Angelico*, in *Revue de l'Art Chrétien*, 1903, pp. 197-200. — Paolo d'ANCONA, *Un ignoto collaboratore dell'Angelico: Zanobi Strozzi*, in *L'Arte*, VIII, 1908, p. 81. — Guglielmo PACCHIONI, *Gli ultimi anni del Beato Angelico*, in *L'Arte*, XII, 1909, pp. 1-4. — Italo MAIONE, *Fra Giovanni Dominici e Beato Angelico*, in *L'Arte*, XVII, 1914, p. 281 ff. & p. 361 ff. — R. van MARLE, *The Development of the Italian Schools of Painting*, vol. X, 1928, p. 52 ff. — Roberto LONGHI, *Un dipinto dell'Angelico a Livorno*, in *Pinacoteca*, I, 1928-1929. — Valerio MARIANI, *Beato Angelico e le "Laudi" del Duecento italiano*, in *Illustrazione Vaticana*, II, 1931, p. 21 ff. — Bernhard BERENSON, *Quadri senza casa, II, Il Quattrocento Fiorentino*, in *Dedalo*, XII, 1932, p. 512 ff.; id., *Italian Pictures of the Renaissance*, Oxford 1932; id., *Pitture Italiane del Rinascimento*, Milan 1936. — Roberto LONGHI, *Fatti di Masolino e di Masaccio*, in *La Critica d'Arte*, 1940, p. 163 ff. — Curt GLASER, *The Louvre Coronation and the Early Phase of Fra Angelico's Art*, in *Gazette des Beaux-Arts*, 1942, pp. 149-164. — Mario SALMI, *Problemi dell'Angelico*, in *Commentari*, X, 1950, pp. 75-81 & 146-156.

INDEX AND BIOGRAPHICAL NOTICES

Notices refer to historical figures mentioned in the text

Acta Sanctorum (original edition Ant-werp-Tongerloo-Brussels, 63 vols., 1643-1902) 108.

ALBERTI Leon Battista (1404?-1472) 16, 17, 21, 23, 24, 26, 27, 29, 57, 63, 108, 113; *De Architectura* 108; *De Statua* 50; *On the Care of the Family* 63, 68; *Treatise on Painting* 57, 108.

ALEXANDER V, Antipope (1409-1410) 8.

ALHAZEN (Ibn Alhasan) 20.
Arabian mathematician, born at Basra late in the 10th century, died in Cairo in 1038. Though many of his writings were inspired by Aristotle, he did much original work in the fields of optics and geometry and enjoyed a great reputation in mediaeval Europe, particularly in Italy. His treatise on optics was translated into Latin by Witelo (1270), whose own treatise on perspective largely derived from Alhazen's conclusions.

ANGELICO Fra, Altarpieces and pre-della scenes:
The Virgin and Child enthroned with Twelve Angels (Frankfort) 37;
Madonna della Stella (Florence) 40;
The Annunciation and the Adoration (Florence, reliquary panels from Santa Maria Novella) 40;
Annunciation (Cortona) 18, 35, 36, 40, 45; Predella 49, 54: *The Marriage of the Virgin* 39, 46; *The Visitation* 41/43, 45, 46; *The Adoration of the Magi* 45, 46; *The Presentation in the Temple* 46, 47; *The Death of the Virgin* 46.
Annunciation (1432, lost) 8.

Linaiuoli Triptych (Florence) 8, 17, 46, 48, 49, 55; Predella 61: *The Adoration of the Magi* 50; *The Martyrdom of St Mark* 51, 54; *St Peter preaching* 54.
The Naming of John the Baptist (Florence) 53, 55.
St James the Great freeing Hermogenes (Paris) 54.
The Virgin enthroned with St Mark, St John the Baptist, St John the Evangelist and Mary Magdalen (Cortona) 55.
The Virgin and Child enthroned with Angels between Sts Dominic, Nicholas of Bari, John the Baptist and Catherine of Alexandria (Perugia) 8, 31, 55, 56, 57, 58; Predella, *Scenes from the Life of St Nicholas of Bari* 60, 67; *The Birth of St Nicholas of Bari, the Vocation of St Nicholas, St Nicholas and the Three Maidens* (Vatican) 58; *St Nicholas addressing an Imperial Emissary and St Nicholas saving a Ship at Sea* (Vatican) 59/61; *St Nicholas saving Three Men condemned to Death and the Death of St Nicholas* (Perugia) 61.
The Virgin and Child enthroned with Sts Peter Martyr, Cosmas, Damian, John the Evangelist, Lawrence and Francis (Annalena Altarpiece) 61, 64.
The Coronation of the Virgin (Louvre) 19, 62, 64, 65, 66, 67, 100, 101; Predella (by Fra Angelico and his pupils): *St Dominic and his Companions fed by Angels* 68.
The Virgin enthroned with Eight Angels between Sts Lawrence, John the Evangelist, Mark, Cosmas, Damian,

119

First a Dominican monk, then archbishop of Florence, where his kindliness, energy and learning made him a popular and influential figure. Canonized by Pope Adrian VI in 1523. Left a considerable body of philosophical *(Summa theologica)*, historical *(Chronica tripartita)* and devotional writings, the latter intended to uplift the morals of the middle and ruling classes of Florence. His *Opera a ben vivere* was written especially for Dianora Soderini, wife of Lorenzo de' Medici.

ARETINO Pietro (1492-1556) 10, 11.
The most daring and high-handed (and the most immoral) Italian writer of his time. He left five comedies, many sonnets and dialogues, a few devotional works, and innumerable letters, some of them masterpieces of style and satire, addressed to the princes and nobles who feared him and actually vied for his favor.

ARISTOTLE 63, 113.
AVERROES (Ibn Rushd) (1126-1198) 20, 29.
Arabian philosopher born at Cordova, in Spain. One of the chief mediaeval commentators of Aristotle, into whose doctrines he initiated the scholastic philosophers, gaining a wide following among Franciscans and at the University of Paris. However, his half pantheist, half rationalist interpretation of Aristotle was condemned by the Catholic Church, and St Thomas Aquinas stigmatized him as *"peripateticae philosophiae depravator."* All the same, Latin editions of his works were widely read in Italy and Europe throughout the Middle Ages and the Renaissance, and exerted a lasting influence.

BALDINUCCI Filippo 11.
BALDOVINETTI Alesso (1427-1499) 109.
BERENSON B. 45.
Berlin, Kaiser Friedrich Museum 111.
BILIOTTI, *Chronica* 40.
Bosco ai Frati, Convent of San Buonaventura 91.
Brescia, Order of the Servites 8.
BRUNELLESCHI Filippo (1379-1446) 18, 22, 26, 34, 38, 44, 46, 47, 57.
BURDACH K. 77.

Cambridge (U.S.A.), Fogg Art Museum 111.
CATHERINE of SIENA, St (1347-1380) 14.
One of the most lovable of Italian saints, who as a girl of 15 entered the Order of Penance of St Dominic. She devoted her life to the sick and poor and wore herself out in attempts to reform the Church.

She left 383 letters written in a pure and beautiful Tuscan rivaling that of Petrarch. Her confessor and biographer, Raimundo da Capua, initiated the Observant movement within the Dominican Order.
CENNINI Cennino (ca. 1370-ca. 1440) 16, 20, 57.
CIARANFI A. M., article in *L'Arte* 34.
Constance, Council of 8.
Cortona 7, 8, 34, 45;
Church of San Domenico 55;
Museo del Gesù 18, 35, 36, 39, 40/43, 45, 47, 49.

DANTE ALIGHIERI (1265-1321) 26.
Diurnus Dominicalis, miniatures 34.
DOMENICO VENEZIANO (?-1461) 8, 63, 64.
DOMINICI, Blessed Giovanni (1357-1419) 14, 16, 28; *Lucula Noctis* 24.
First a Dominican monk in his native Florence, then archbishop of Ragusa, cardinal and papal envoy in Bohemia, Poland and Hungary, dying at Budapest. A crusading reformer, an inspired orator and writer, he dominated the Dominican Order in the early 15th century; he may be regarded as the spiritual mentor of both St Antoninus and Fra Angelico.
DONATELLO (1386-1466) 26, 29, 34.
DOUGLAS L. 45.

EUGENIUS IV, Pope (1431-1437) 83.
Born Gabriele Condolmieri in Venice in 1383, elected pope under the name of Eugenius IV in 1431. He was not recognized by the Council of Basel, who renewed the Schism by electing the Duke of Savoy, Amédée VIII, as Antipope Felix V. Eugenius labored

incessantly to restore church unity and reform the monastic orders, and was an enlightened patron of the arts and humanist learning.

Early Italian poet, born at Todi, near Assisi. Studied law at the University of Bologna, then successfully practised as " clerk " and public officer at Todi. After the sudden death of his wife about 1268, he gave everything he owned to the poor and became a mendicant friar, writing and singing " lauds " to God in penitence for his sins and those of all mankind.

Founder of the political power of the house of Medici in Florence. The shrewdest of businessmen and politicians, Cosimo was also a man of genuine culture and a great connoisseur, patronizing Ghiberti, Donatello, Brunelleschi, Luca della Robbia, Michelozzo and many other artists.

CONTENTS

ON THE TITLE PAGE

Angel's Head, detail from the Coronation of the Virgin. Ca. 1430-1440. Louvre, Paris.

ON THE JACKET

Head of the Virgin, detail from the Coronation of the Virgin. Ca. 1430-1440. Louvre, Paris.
The Descent from the Cross, detail from the left side. Ca. 1440. Museo di San Marco, Florence.

THIS VOLUME
THE TENTH OF THE COLLECTION

THE TASTE OF OUR TIME

WAS PRINTED
BOTH TEXT AND COLORPLATES
BY THE

SKIRA

COLOR STUDIO
AT IMPRIMERIES RÉUNIES S.A., LAUSANNE
FINISHED THE TWENTIETH DAY OF FEBRUARY
NINETEEN HUNDRED AND FIFTY-FIVE

THE PLATES WERE ENGRAVED BY
GUEZELLE ET RENOUARD, PARIS

*The works reproduced in this volume were photographed by Claudio Emmer in Italy,
and by Louis Laniepce in Paris*